Contact!

Contact!

A Book of Encounters

JAN MORRIS

W. W. Norton & Company
New York · London

First published in Great Britain under the title
Contact! A Book of Glimpses

For information about permission to reproduce selections from this
book, write to Permissions, W. W. Norton & Company, Inc.,
500 Fifth Avenue, New York, NY 10110

For information about special discounts for bulk purchases,
please contact W. W. Norton Special Sales at
specialsales@wwnorton.com or 800-233-4830

Manufacturing by Courier Westford
Production manager: Anna Oler

Library of Congress Cataloging-in-Publication Data

Morris, Jan, 1926–
Contact! : a book of encounters / Jan Morris.
p. cm.
Includes index.
ISBN 978-0-393-07640-0 (hardcover)
1. Morris, Jan, 1926– —Travel. 2. Voyages and travels. I. Title.
G465M658 2009
910.4092—dc22   2009052193

W. W. Norton & Company, Inc.
500 Fifth Avenue, New York, N.Y. 10110
www.wwnorton.com

W. W. Norton & Company Ltd.
Castle House, 75/76 Wells Street, London W1T 3QT

1 2 3 4 5 6 7 8 9 0

Dedicated to the whole lot of them

Introductory

‘Contact’ is a noun of varied nuances, not all to my taste. Ambitious businessmen make useful contacts at golf clubs or race meetings. Diplomats and journalists are urged to cultivate their contacts. Spies have contacts and so do publicity executives, and people with poor eyesight. On the other hand contacts turn the lights on, start the engine, send the rocket off, launch the movie Spitfires into glory, and it is this meaning of the word that gives me the title of this album.

In a lifetime of travel and literature I have written relatively little about people. Places, atmospheres, histories have figured far more in my all too often purple prose. But people everywhere, nevertheless, have been sparks of my work, if often only in glimpses – a sighting through a window, a gentle snatch of sound, the touch of a hand – and it is mostly such fugitive moments and observations, scattered across half a century and forty-odd books, that I have here gratefully plucked out of their literary obscurity.

Often I have given them only a few lines, or a paragraph; occasionally the people have known me as James rather than Jan, because until 1972 I wrote in the persona of James Morris; but my fleeting contacts with them have fuelled my travels down the years, generated my motors, excited my

1

laughter and summoned my sympathies. I write of them here more or less as I wrote of them at the time, and I recall them not in any chronological or geographical order, but jumbled. Their locations will generally be self-evident, and I have included dates only when they seem essential to the historical sense of the piece. Otherwise all these encounters simply occurred between Here and There, to Him or Her, after Then and before Now.

Rich and poor people are remembered here, young and old, grand and humble, primitive and exquisitely civilized, named and anonymous, in the particular and in the general. Every one of them, of course, deserves more than the handful of words I have resurrected in these pages: but there it is, they are seldom friends or even acquaintances, only contacts.

Trefan Morys, 2009

Contact!

A sighting in Texas

On my fourth day in the city
I looked through the window
and saw a dreamlike figure sauntering by.
He had a sack over his arm, and a stick over his
shoulder,
and he wore a high-crowned hat and a cloak, I think,
and he strolled past easy, insolent and amused.
My heart leapt to see him.
'Who was that?' I cried, rushing to the window,
'that man with the stick, and the high-crowned hat,
and the sack on his arm?'
My hostess returned me reprovingly to our
conversation.
'I saw nobody,' she sweetly and carefully said.
'But tell me, have you had time to see our new Picasso
in the Fine Arts Museum?
And will you have an opportunity to meet with
Mrs Oveta Culp Hobby?'

Manhattan dialogue

⌒

I chanced one day, off the joggers' circuit in Central Park, to come across a young black man fast asleep upon a bench below the lake. His overcoat was thrown over him, his books were placed neatly side by side upon the ground. His head upon his clasped hands, as in kindergarten plays, he was breathing regularly and gently, as though bewitched. Even as I watched, a grey squirrel, skipping across the green, leapt across his legs to the back of the bench, where it sat tremulously chewing, and almost at the same time there arose a brisk gust of wind, tangy with salt.

A scatter of leaves and fallen blossoms came with it, flicked and eddied around the bench. The squirrel paused, twitched and vanished. The black man opened his eyes, as the breeze dusted his face, and, seeing me standing there bemused, smiled me a slow sleepy smile. 'Be not afeared,' I said ridiculously, on the spur of the moment, 'the isle is full of noises.'

'Yeah,' the man replied, stretching and scratching mightily in the morning. 'Bugs, too.'

At the hotel door

⌒

I was going out through the door of the Albergo Savoia
Excelsior in Trieste when a man simultaneously entered. We
bumped into one another, our bags and luggage got mixed
up, and we both apologized. He was a theatrical-looking
character, with a camel coat slung over his shoulders – perhaps one of the opera singers from the Teatro Verdi. When
we had disentangled ourselves he stood there for a moment,
motionless.

'Where are you from?' he said.

'Wales.'

'Wales! How *wonderful*!'

Oh you splendid liar, I said to myself, you've never heard
of the place. There was a pause. I laughed, and so did he. He
shook my hand in both of his. We lingered for a moment
and parted. When I think of Trieste, lust and love I often
think of him.

Self-discipline

⌒

At Kanpur, in India, I came across a man with whom I felt an
instant affinity. That he was deeply unhappy was obvious,
but he numbed his misery by touching things. Day and night
he wandered the streets of the city, earnestly and methodic-
ally touching windows, doorposts, lamp standards, apparently to strict unwritten rules. Sometimes he appeared to feel
that he had neglected his task, and did a street all over again,
paying a still more diligent attention to the doorknobs. I
spoke to him one morning, but he responded only with an

engaging preoccupied smile, as if to say that, although some other time it would be delightful to have a chat, that day he simply hadn't a moment to spare.

Honesty

Sometimes Sydney seems to be inhabited chiefly by school-children, children kicking pebbles across bridges, children racing fig leaves down the channels of ornamental fountains, children clambering like invading armies all over the Opera House, or mustered in their thousands in the New South Wales Art Gallery. They seem to me a stalwart crew. 'Now this is a Picasso,' I heard a teacher say in the gallery one day. 'I'm sure you all know who Picasso was.' 'I don't,' piped up a solitary small Australian at the back, and I bowed to him as the only absolutely honest soul in sight.

Not Chopin

When communism failed in Poland, materialism took over. There were bright new shops, posh hotels, plenty of cars, all the usual paraphernalia of capitalism. 'Nice car,' I remarked one day to the man who drove me to the airport in his big new Volvo. He shrugged his shoulders and looked at me with a dry smile. I knew what he meant. 'Well, no,' I added in afterthought, 'I suppose it's not Chopin'; and he knew what I meant, too.

After the ball was over

Not so long ago the chief celebrants of the legendary Venetian carnival were the children of Venice, who bought their funny faces and moustaches from the chain stores and emerged to saunter self-consciously through the city in fancy dress.

On the final evening of the festivities I was walking home when I saw before me, in a hurried glimpse, three small figures crossing a square from one lane to another. In the middle walked a thin little man, his overcoat rather too long for him and buttoned down the front, his gloves very neat, his hat very precise, his shoes very polished. Clutching his right hand was a tiny Pierrot, his orange pom-pom waggling in the half-light. Clutching his left hand was a minuscule fairy, her legs wobbly in white cotton, her skirt infinitesimal, her wand warped a little with the excitement and labour of the day. Quickly, silently and carefully they crossed the square and disappeared from view; the fairy had to skip a bit to keep up, the Pierrot cherished a sudden determination to walk only on the lines between the paving stones, and the man trod a precarious tightrope between the indulgent and the conventional.

How small they looked, and respectable, I thought to myself! How carefully their mother had prepared them, all three, to survive the scrutiny of their neighbours! How thin a reflection they offered of Venice's rumbustious carnivals of old, her Doges and masked patriciate, her grand lovers, her tall warships and her princely artists! How touching the little Venetians, tight buttoned in their alleyways!

The student's request

In the shadowy underneath of a bridge in Isfahan a student sits, dangling his feet over a sluice and reading a book. His face is dark and meditative, and his air of poetic concentration is all one asks of a Persian student. He has caught sight of us, in a dreamy sort of way, and as he buttons his jacket, gathers his notebooks and moves sidelong in our direction, we recognize one of the more endearing hazards of modern travel, the Student of English. We are too late to escape. 'Sir!' he cries. 'Madam!' fluttering his notes and bearing down on us. 'Allow me please to ask you one question, before you leave the bridge: is it permissible or not, in the English language, to pursue a gerund with a participle? And would you be kind enough to comment on my pronunciation in the following passage, Exercise 12? Sit down, sir; sit down, madam! Be comfortable!'

Déjà entendu!

On a winter day in Zagreb a man bundled in a greatcoat is playing an instrument of his own invention, consisting of rows of wine and mineral-water bottles strung on a contraption rather like a washing line and tuned by their varying contents of liquid. He is playing with great delicacy a piece I know well, but can't for the life of me place, and around him a smiling crowd has gathered, amused by the instrument, touched by the tune. In the front row of the audience a small child of two or three in a woolly blue and white jumper suit, with hat to match, is performing a shuffly sort of dance to the music. I am curiously affected, partly because of the endearing busker, partly because of the sweetly familiar music – oh, and hang on, I think I remember what that tune is. Isn't it one of those charming Fritz Kreisler fripperies they used to play at palm-court cafes, with a lady violinist in a satin blouse, and the grammar-school music master moonlighting at the piano? 'Schön Rosmarin' – isn't that it?

Breath of the woods

A junior functionary all but monopolized my attention during my visit to the Legislature of the Canadian North West Territories at Yellowknife. She was about fifteen years old, I would guess, indeterminately Caucasian, Indian, Inuit or Métis, and tremendous fun. Busy as she was taking perpetual missives from one member to another, bobbing incessantly to the chair en route, she managed to elevate the whole session to a jollier and more sensible level. She laughed to herself and to others, she did her bows with a wonderfully comic jerkiness, she stuck her tongue out at her colleagues, she yawned, she hitched her tights up, she cheerfully swung her legs when she was sitting down and walked in a delightfully insouciant way when she was on her feet. I loved this irrepressible child of the north: the legislators droned on as legislators will, but she brought a breath of the woods inside.

Costa del Sol, 1960s

Sometimes I went out on the beach at Fuengirola to watch

the fishermen at work. It could be heartbreaking to see. They worked like slaves, wading into the sea with their huge heavy net and laboriously hauling it in, inch by inch, hour by hour up the sands: so much depended on the catch, so much labour and good humour had been expended, so many children were waiting to be fed, so many anxious mothers hoping – and when at last the haul appeared, often enough only a dozen small sardines in the mesh of the net, the fishermen carefully cleared up their tackle and dispersed to their homes in weary silence.

Caravan of martyrs

In the summer of 1958 the young King Feisal of Iraq was assassinated, leaving his contemporary and close relative King Hussein of Jordan isolated upon his own threatened throne. I was in Jordan when, a few days later, Hussein made a public declaration about the tragedy. His face was lined and tired, and moisture glistened in the corners of his eyes. Ministers, officials, officers and security guards were grouped behind his chair. Clearing his throat huskily, the King said slowly: 'I have now had confirmation of the murder of my cousin, brother and childhood playmate, King Feisal of Iraq, and all his royal family.' He paused, his eyes filling, his lip trembling, a muscle working rhythmically in the side of his jaw, and then he said it again, in identical words, but in a voice that was awkwardly thickening. 'I have now received confirmation of the murder of my cousin, brother and childhood playmate, King Feisal of Iraq, and all his royal family.' And raising his head from his notes,

Hussein added in his strange formal English: 'They are only the last in a caravan of martyrs.'

Trial of an alleged spy

The court sat on a kind of stage against a background of opaque white curtains. In the centre were the military judge and his two assessors, generals all, immaculate in dove grey and sitting in their tall wooden chairs like bulky Buddhas. To the left sat the prosecutor, the procurator-general of the Soviet Union, a heavy and formidable lawyer in a sombre blue uniform. The lights were blinding – chandeliers, strings of bulbs, floodlight, cameramen's flashlights, bathing the whole scene in chill brilliance and giving the members of the court a waxen cosmetic look. Punctually at ten Gary Powers was led in with an escort of two young soldiers in olive-green jackets and blue trousers. He wore a blue Russian suit too large for him, so that he had to hitch up his sleeves now and then, and they put him in the wooden dock, like a big child's playpen beneath the floodlights, and the sentries stood at attention beside it as beside a catafalque. Powers was obviously frightened, and so was I.

The one left behind

Through the windows of a lakeside restaurant at Mölln I watch four German children playing. Their families are lunching inside, and I would judge the children to be between six and ten years old. The two boys are always in the lead, dashing about the lake, the girls follow enthusiastically behind. One is slim, blonde and pretty, and wears a floral dress she likes to flounce about. The other is plain and plump, and wears a blue anorak, with sleeves too long for her, over a short tartan skirt. The plain girl is always last. She can never quite keep up. When they run out to the end of the jetty, she is always left behind. When they rush helter-skelter into the restaurant to speak to their families, the door closes behind the other three and there is a long pause before, panting heavily, the short fat girl opens it again with difficulty and stumbles in. I like her best of the quartet – she tries so hard, laughs so gamely, struggles so constantly to tuck up the sleeves of her anorak. I feel for her, too. However when they all scamper out of the restaurant again, and I offer her a smile as she passes my table, she returns a most malevolent glare.

Haute couture

⌒

I was invited to write about one of the Paris summer collections for an American magazine, and sat incongruously in the front row among the condescending New York buyers and unbelievably ugly princesses of American fashion journalism. How awful they looked, draped in their furs, red taloned, emaciated to the point of grotesqueness, while all about them graceful exponents of the art of French allure glided silkily around the room and along the catwalk. The audience otherwise seemed to be composed chiefly of characters from Proust.

'I've always said,' observed one American matron to another, 'I'm not going to be a possessive mother, because *his* was' – and she jerked her head in the direction of her husband in the next seat. The two ladies eyed him speculatively. 'He'll be no good to us in Venice,' said the other. 'He'll be lost with those gondolier people.'

Young English wife, on her honeymoon, I guessed: 'Oh, look at the castle. Isn't that a lovely castle?' Young English husband: 'It's a castle. A castle is a castle. You've seen castles before.' She relapsed into thoughtful silence. He returned to his thriller.

Said an American man, to me: 'You gotta read this book. I've been reading it all the way since London. It's called *God Owns My Business*. *God Owns My Business*, that's the title. The guy who wrote it, he's a very low-key man, but he's got a sign above his store, "Christ Is My Manager". When do we get to Innsbruck? We might get a hamburger there.'

If you prick us?

I shared a taxi one day with a lady in a blue silk turban, who was visiting Washington and was about to meet her daughter for lunch at a Hot Shoppe. Down the great thoroughfares we drove, and all the memorials of the American splendour passed us one by one, granite and concrete, obelisk and colonnade. My companion drew my attention now and then to a White House or a Treasury, but it was as we passed the

Capitol itself, and were deploring the state of the world in general, that she spoke the words I best remember: 'I sometimes wonder, oh, what kind of a world are we bringing our children into, when you have to pay a quarter for a doughnut?'

Twenty-five cents for a doughnut! Even Americans bleed.

The sprig of rosemary

I was driving along a road in Portugal when I spied a tray of oranges for sale outside a cottage. It was blazing hot, and I stopped to buy some. Nobody attended the fruit, so I selected three oranges for myself and knocked on the cottage door. Nobody came. There was no sign of life. I peered through the window, I walked around the back, and in the end I opened the front door. It was very dark inside, but when my eyes accustomed themselves I saw that fast asleep in a corner of the room was a small old lady. I coughed and shuffled my feet, and without a start she awoke. Her very first reaction was to smile. Her second was to reach for her straw hat on a nearby chair and put it carefully on her head. She accepted my few coins for the oranges but then, hustling me kindly outside, took two apricots from another box and gave me them as a present. All the time she smiled, and bustled around looking for other kindnesses to perform. When we had said goodbye, and I had returned to the car, she came running out of the garden gate again, smiling still, clutching her hat on her head, to give me a sprig of rosemary.

Different responses

My family and I lived for a time near the Swiss frontier in France. On the French side the gendarmes were jolly, careless, and often had wine on their breaths. On the Swiss side the police were cool, diligent, courteous and unsmiling. My car in those days was a Rolls-Royce, grand, decorative and elderly. The French gendarmes were delightedly amused by this vehicle, and sometimes asked permission to sit at its wheel, or try the squashy grey leather seats behind. To the Swiss border police, on the other hand, a Rolls-Royce was an image of wealth, and a quaint middle-aged example like mine, not old enough to be a valuable antique, certainly not new enough to be a status symbol, seemed to confuse their responses. They habitually greeted us with a mixture of respect and condescension, covering all contingencies.

Flying the flag

The Aboriginal flag of gold, black and yellow was hoisted above Sydney Town Hall, but was soon pulled down again. By the time I reached the park the Aboriginal Day rally seemed to have fizzled out, too, and all I found was a small huddle of dark-skinned people around an open bonfire, surrounded by litter on the edge of the green. They greeted me with wan concern, offering me beer out of an ice bucket, sidling around me rather and occasionally winking. A small thin boy with cotton wool stuffed in one ear wandered here and there leading a black puppy on a string. Others kicked a football about in the gathering dusk. A strong smell of alcohol hung over us, and the man with the bucket urged me quietly, again and again, to have one for the road. Had the rally been a success? I asked. 'Yeah,' they said, and looked into the fire.

The Frenchest person

The Frenchest person I ever met was Yves Saint-Laurent, the couturier. He was utterly French. He told me that the only books he ever read were eleven volumes of Proust's *À la recherche du temps perdu*, over and over again, but that the twelfth and last volume he had never read at all – saving it up, I suppose, for a last splurge of Frenchness on his deathbed chaise longue. Everything that was French seemed to be embodied in him, even a bit of the old *gloire*, for there was a distinctly grand manner lurking behind his melancholy shyness, and he lived in a grand style too. Saint-Laurent liked to call himself an artisan, and the little world of craftspeople he had built up around him, the dedicated world of cutters, shoemakers, milliners and tailors, seemed to me a true ornament of French civilization, and a vindication of French pride. He told me that all I needed for elegance was one dress, a pair of jeans, some blouses and a raincoat. I asked him if he was consciously contributing to the splendour of France, and he smiled rather distantly. He was, he said, he was.

A fine scoundrel

ᴗᴗ

A celebrated, or notorious, rebel leader in Oman was Suleiman bin Hamyar, who owned the only motorcar in the Green Mountains. I saw him arriving in it one day for a political parley at the village of Nizwa, and the sight of his American convertible careening recklessly out of the roadless mountains was wonderfully inspiriting. The roof of the car was closed, but on the boot there sat a Negro slave, armed with a rifle, with his feet sticking through the back window into the inside of the car; and when it stopped this slave jumped off like lightning, as promptly and neatly as any duke's footman, and opened the door with a flourish.

I walked across to meet the old sheikh, and he greeted me with an expression of unfathomable foxiness, suggesting to me instantly some infinitely clever beast in Aesop, about to hoodwink a goat. Suleiman was a big man with a powerful face, rather Dickensian in concept, and a triangular grey beard. On his head was a twisted blue and white turban. His aba was blue, gold-edged and filmy. In his hand was a cane with a carved end, on his belt a curved dagger of splendid ostentation.

My own instincts told me that this fine scoundrel should be instantly decapitated, for the public good, but I was rather glad, all the same, when he later reappeared from the parley intact, and was driven away into his mountains with only minor (and I felt sure temporary) modifications of his manner.

Enjoy yourself!

It took many hours, on a Sunday evening, to drive from Trieste the few miles into Tito's Yugoslavia. I can see now the hundreds of cars lurching and overheating in the gathering dusk, the ad hoc hamburger bars beside the road, the occasional truck bullying its way up the queue by sheer weight and horsepower, pale weary faces at the windows of buses and at last the dim-lit frontier post, and a joyless official with a red star on his cap. A slow flicking through the pages of our passports, a silent gesture of release, and away with us into the communist half of Europe. 'Cheer up,' I said to the frontier official once. 'Enjoy yourself,' the man lugubriously replied.

The helmsman

Our helmsman, although he is surrounded by talkative friends and relatives of all ages, is ever attentive to his craft and courteously watchful of me: and sometimes, indeed, sailing in such a ramshackle sampan crablike against the current from one island to another, to the laboured chugging of diesel engines and the creaking of timbers – sometimes I feel I would like to be assimilated into Chineseness myself, and sail these waters under Chinese helmsmanship for good.

A literary test

In Newfoundland in those days it was necessary to find a guarantor before one could cash foreign money orders.

Knowing nobody in town, and finding that the public library had a copy of a book of mine about Venice, I introduced myself to the librarian and asked her to endorse a travellers' cheque. How could she confirm, she sensibly demanded, that I was who I said I was? By a simple literary test, I suggested: surely nobody else on earth could recite by heart the last line of my book on Venice, which she had upon her own shelves.

Solemnly she reached for the volume. Nervously I stood at her desk while she turned to the final page, and ran her eye down the paragraph to the end of it. 'Well?' she said. I cleared my throat. The concluding words of my book were not very stately. 'No wonder,' I mumbled then, feeling distinctly disadvantaged, 'No wonder George Eliot's husband fell into the Grand Canal.' Without a flicker that librarian of old St John's closed the book, returned it to the shelf and authorized my money.

Judgement

'What's this?' demanded a Soviet customs official curtly one day, extracting a typescript from my baggage and simultaneously eyeing my then epicene figure. 'It's a psychological novel,' said I. 'Oh, a *psychological novel*,' he replied in a voice of infinite understanding, as though I had shared a confidence with him; and carefully repacking the script in my suitcase, he waved me through.

Byronic

A symbolic figure of the South African tragedy in the years of apartheid was Christopher Gell, one of the most inspiring of the liberal activists, whose name was almost legendary, who was a unique source of guidance and information, and who lived as it happens in an iron lung. From there he cocked a perpetual snook at the Afrikaner Nationalists. A well-trodden path led to his little house, and brought a constant stream of people interested in the African Risorgimento, and anxious to meet this strange Byronic figure.

Gell received them in his lung. He was tall, painfully cadaverous, immensely vivacious. He wore glasses and had one arm suspended above him in a kind of sling. Books and elaborate filing cabinets lined the room, and his table was littered with proofs and pamphlets and letters. Often the telephone rang and Gell launched himself into a farrago of opinion, prejudice and argument till the voice of the man at the other end of the line sounded breathless and dispirited, Gell's face was wickedly aglow and the conversation ended in intellectual annihilation.

Then he turned to you. 'Now then, let me put you straight about these bloody Nats.' He presented his case with tremendous energy, witty, outrageous, caustic, irrepressible, pausing sometimes to scribble a name down for you or dash off a note of introduction, swearing, joking, laughing, in a most extraordinary flood of stimulation and conviction. Slowly, though, his damaged physique ran down. His breathing became gasping and spasmodic, his face more strained with effort, and the gusto drained from his body before your eyes, like the symbolism of a Gothic painting. He would still be talking as you left him, though, and his anxious humorous eyes would be looking at you in the little mirror above his head. 'Of course we're intolerant,' he would say as you left him. 'We have to be. We'd never get anywhere with these stiffs if we weren't.'

Doubly damned

At the Rock Hotel in Gibraltar I overheard two very old-school American matrons commenting upon the grumpy hotel porter who had just dumped their bags unceremoniously on the lobby floor. 'What an unpleasant man!' said one. 'What can you expect?' responded the other. 'He is British, my dear, and *male*.'

Dung and diplomacy

One day I walked up to the royal palace in Brussels, and just as I arrived a plenipotentiary emerged from its gates in a big black car after a diplomatic presentation to the King of the Belgians. A footling squadron of cavalry awaited him in the ceremonial square outside. Its officers wore romantic white cloaks. Its troopers, in slightly cockeyed bearskins, as in musical comedies, included some sceptical-looking horsemen of the old-sweat school, and at least one rosy-cheeked woman. When they clattered and bounced away with the ambassadorial Cadillac, a municipal road-sweeping truck came trundling around the place where they had mustered, cleaning up the horse shit. Its driver told me he spent his days doing it. There were so many embassies, missions and international institutions in Brussels, he said, that the palace cavalry was always at it – and sure enough, as he spoke, the horsepersons, having disappeared round the corner with their fluttering lances, came ridiculously back again with another couple of limousines.

Steamboat Gothic

Longwood is the oddest of the mansions of Natchez, Mississippi, where Southern myth and prejudice are very powerful. The house was begun shortly before the Civil War, a wild architectural extravaganza, and Northern workmen were brought in to work upon it. Soon after the war began they dropped their tools and left, leaving the house unfinished to this day, with their hammers and wheelbarrows and paintboxes still lying about, ladders propped against walls, scaffolding still in place. Octagonal, domed and balconied, it stands in a wooded garden as a grotesque monument of Steamboat Gothic, its glassless windows gaping. Only the ground floor is inhabitable, and in it there lives all alone Mr John Price, white-haired and nearsighted, who once entertained us to a very enjoyable lunch.

This was a feat, for he seems usually to live entirely on marshmallows and fig rolls, but a jolly cousin of his came in to do the cooking, and the results were capital. Mr Price had no tablecloth handy, but a sheet on the table served just as well, and we ate Southern fried chicken in enormous quantities, and blancmange and cheese, finishing with either fig rolls or marshmallows, I forget which.

War story

An Australian boy once told me that his father had recently taken part in a military parade. 'What kind of a hat did he wear?' I asked for something to say. One of those hats, he replied, which were flat on one side but turned up in the other. 'I know,' I said, 'like they used to wear in the Great War.' There was a silence for a moment, and then the boy spoke. 'I *hate* the Great War,' he said, and my heart turned.

Chinese jingles

Early in a performance I attended in one of the regime's Children's Palaces, by an orchestra of children under the age of five, the virtuoso lead xylophonist happened to get herself a full tone out of key. She never appeared to notice. Nor did any of the other performers, all dimples, winsome smiles and bobbing heads up there on the stage. On they went in fearful discord, tinkle-tinkle, clang-clang, simpering smugly to the end.

At El Kharga

El Kharga is one of the five isolated oases which lie well to the west of the Nile in the Egyptian desert, and it has always been a place of exile. Nestorius was banished there, and Athanasius too, it is said. In our time political prisoners are immured in a detention camp at the oasis, and I once encountered some of them. They were patients in the local hospital, lying on straw palliasses on the floor of a bare ward. A murderous lot they looked, all the more sinister because bandages and plasters covered their eyes and supported their limbs – one and all were enemies of the state, and their interrogations had not been easy. I talked to them warily of this and that, the conditions of their detention and their hopes of release, and they told me that every morning they were given a lecture of indoctrination by a representative of the regime. Something in their eyes, though, told me they were far from brainwashed, and now and then a particularly savage old dissident lying in a corner intervened with a caustic witticism, delivered in the most cultured of English accents and with the bite of an incisive mind. Thus Nestorius might have spoken, I thought, during his exile at El Kharga.

The European

I met a man so allegorically Dutch that I deliberately engaged him in what I hoped would be allegorically Dutch conversation. He was a tall man with military moustaches, deep-blue eyes and a proper burgher's paunch, but he did not talk about Rembrandt, tulips, dykes, the German occupation, Queen Beatrix, the new season's herrings, Admiral de Ruyter or what was playing at the Concertgebouw that evening. No. He talked about unemployment, too many Asian immigrants, keeping his weight down and his hopes, earlier in life, of being a professional footballer. He was a citizen of the Netherlands, but I have met him all over western Europe, and that's what he always talks about.

The most dramatic as well as the most diligent conductor in the world is to be seen in action at the Theatre of Opera and Ballet in Odessa. He is an elderly man, but passionate. All around him as he works peculiar things are happening. Behind, in the half-empty auditorium, a constant buzz of homely conversation underlies the score, and three ill-shaven Levantines in the second row seem to be in the throes of opium dreams, squirming and sighing in their seats. In front, the stage is alive with minor mishaps – trap-doors mysteriously closing and opening, fans being dropped, iron accessories clattering, while the cast of *La Traviata* smile resolutely across the footlights with a treasury of gold teeth.

The conductor is unperturbed. Majestically he sails through the confusions of the evening, impervious to them all, sometimes grunting emotionally, sometimes joining in an aria in a powerful baritone, throwing his fine head back, bending double, conspiratorially withdrawing, pugnaciously advancing, with infinite variations of facial expression and frequent hissed injunctions to the woodwind. Nobody in the socialist bloc fulfils a norm more devotedly.

The choice

'Are you a man or a woman?' asked the Fijian taxi driver as he drove me from the airport.

'I am a respectable, rich, middle-aged English widow,' I replied.

'Good,' he said, 'just what I want,' and put his hand upon my knee.

A Gypsy kiss

~

In the evening the entire population of Tirana seemed to emerge for the twilight passeggiata, strolling up and down the main avenue, sitting on the edges of fountains, milling around funfairs, wandering haphazardly across highways. I loved the louche insouciance of it all, the immense hum over everything, the quirks and surprises. Once I felt a small dry kiss on my arm, and turned to find a Gypsy child irresistibly importuning me for cash.

Understanding the truth

~

What would happen, I asked a fundamentalist predicant of the Dutch Reformed Church in South Africa, if an African walked into one of his services?

'I would have him removed. My church is for Europeans, and it would be wrong to allow a native to worship there. God divided the races for His own purposes, and it is not for us to doubt His wisdom.'

'Or if a Chinaman turned up one day, or an Eskimo?'

'No, my church is not for Asiatics. I would send them away. But now you must not misunderstand me,' he added earnestly, tapping his knee with his forefinger. 'I don't say they shouldn't have a service at all. If there was no other church for them to attend I would hold a service myself, not inside my church, of course, but in a field if necessary. I feel this very strongly: that no man, whatever his colour, whatever his race, wheresoever he cometh from, should be deprived of the opportunity of worshipping Him who is the creator of us all.'

As I left the house the predicant clasped my arm, rather in the Rotarian manner, and pointed across the street outside, where an elderly black woman was hobbling out of a shop, screaming something in a searing treble over her shoulder. She crossed the pavement, closed one nostril with her finger and emptied her nose noisily into the gutter. Then, wiping her nose with her skirt, she turned round, still screeching, and disappeared indoors.

'You see?' said the predicant. 'My dear friend, we are not unkindly, but you must live among them to understand the Truth.'

Social status in the people's dictatorship

Mrs Wang had invited me to lunch at her Shanghai apartment, but it gave me no culture shock. True, we ate eggs in aspic, a kind of pickled small turnip and strips of a glutinous substance which suggested to me jellified seaweed, and Mrs Wang evoked for me her hysterectomy by acupuncture ('When they slit me open, oh, it hurt very bad, but after it was very *strange* feeling, very *strange* . . .') – nevertheless her home seemed to me the bourgeois home par excellence. It had the statutory upright piano, a picture of two kittens playing with a ball of wool, a bookshelf of paperbacks and a daily help. It had a daughter who had come over to help cook lunch, and a husband away at the office who sent his regards. 'We are very lucky,' said kind Mrs Wang. 'We have a certain social status.'

Baleful eyes

No infidel is allowed to enter the most celebrated shrine of Kerbala, the holy city of the Shias in Iraq, but I knocked at the door of a neighbouring house and asked if I might climb to its roof to see into its courtyard. The owner of the house was all smiles, but it turned out to be a simple inn, catering for pilgrims from Iraq, and as I walked up its narrow winding staircase I found myself passing a series of sparsely furnished rooms – a bed and a prayer mat and a hard cold floor. In each of these doorless cells there was a pilgrim, and as I climbed my way up those steep steps each turned his baleful eyes in my direction. I shall never forget the detestation that overcame the faces of those merciless old men when they observed an infidel on the stairs, nor the relief with which at last I escaped the gamut of their loathing and emerged upon the roof, with the golden dome of the mosque in front of me and the wide sunlit courtyard, crowded with robed pilgrims, spread before me like a chessboard.

Passing the nut

I was trekking alone between Namche Bazaar and Thangboche, in the Nepali Himalaya. I was walking fast, in pleasant heathland country, and presently I saw far ahead of

31

me another solitary figure, moving in the same direction. It was a robust Sherpa woman, wearing long aprons and a high embroidered hat. Despite her hampering skirts she, too, was making good time, striding firmly along the track, but gradually I overhauled her until, in a narrow bend of the path, I was able to overtake her.

She had given no sign that she knew of my presence, never turning round or looking over her shoulder, just ploughing steadily on like a colourful battleship. As I passed her, however, her left hand suddenly shot into mine. For a moment we touched. Neither of us spoke, and I was too surprised to stop, but I felt some small hard object pass from her hand into mine.

I looked down to see what it was, passed so strangely from traveller to traveller, and found it was a small brown nut. When I turned round to thank her for it, she grinned and nodded and waved me on; so I pushed ahead up the hill, cracking its shell between my teeth.

The master glass-blower

Here stands the master glass-blower of Murano, in the Venetian lagoon. He stands grandly assured beside his furnace, watched by a wondering tour group, with a couple of respectful apprentices to hand him his implements, and his long pipe in his hand like a wand. With a flourish he raises it to his lips, and with a gentle blow produces a small round bubble of glass. A twist, a chip, another delicate breath, and there appears the embryo of an ornament. A twiddle of the pipe follows, a slice with an iron rod, a dollop of molten glass, a swift plunge into the fire, a gulp or two, a flourish in the air, a sudden snap of iron shears – and abruptly the glass-blower lays down his work with a gesture of artistic exhaustion, leaving the apprentice boys around him silent with respect, and the tourists, sweating in the heat, clustered awestruck about a huge glass harlequin, beady eyed and multicoloured, whose long spindly legs, swollen stomach, drunken grin and dissipated attitude breathe a spirit of unsurpassable vulgarity.

An official of the glass factory shouts through the window to a pair of husbands who have evaded the tour, and are sitting comfortably on the quay outside. 'Gentlemen! Gentlemen!' he calls reprovingly. 'Sirs! Your charming ladies are awaiting you in the vestibule. All the prices are marked!'

Awful, really

A hand touched my shoulder as I stood watching a crowd of masked and black-robed women crowding around a water hole in the Omani village of Ibri. 'You shouldn't stand about here, you know,' a voice said in English, 'you might catch something. The sanitation is ever so bad!' It was an Omani Christian convert, product of a mission school somewhere, whom I had met earlier that day.

He invited me to visit his nearby house. It stood behind a heavy gate, for there was ever such bad robbers in Ibri, he said, and as we entered I saw, half hidden in a dim and smoky recess, four or five black-shrouded figures almost motionless, and soundless but for a few moaning noises. I did not like to ask what was happening in there, but as we climbed the stairs my companion remarked casually, hitching up his shroud: 'That's my wife. She's got something wrong with her inside, so a few friends came in to look after her.'

We sat pleasantly in an upstairs room, watching the passers-by from a window and eating some rather stringy pomegranates. Yes, he sighed, Ibri was a funny place. The people was very funny. 'It's awful, really,' concluded the apostate, removing a pip from between his two front teeth.

Changing the guard

Every other morning they change the guard outside the Presidential Palace in Santiago. An enormous military band plays, and the two guard companies, equipped with high boots, swords and resplendent spurs, march and counter-march with an almost ominous certainty. This is no toy-soldier parade. It feels all too real, as though the participating soldiery, dropping to firing positions by the flick of a command, might easily exterminate each other by numbers. It ends happily, though, for when the ceremony is over the two young subalterns of the guard, marvellously slim and elegant, salute each other with brisk respect, shake hands like brothers and stride off together into the palace. There is a moment or two of silence and then the band strikes up a waltz, and even the undemonstrative Chileans, standing woodenly all about, tap an occasional tight-laced toe.

Looking after the place

I was once driving through the Transvaal when I noticed a small obelisk on a hillock beside the road. I stopped, and found beside it an old Afrikaner farmer, crouched in what seemed to be silent meditation. He wore an unbuttoned waterproof jacket. A linen hat slouched around his ears and a mass of curly hair lay down his neck and oozed over his collar. He turned to look at me, and I found myself gazing into the bluest and clearest and hardest pair of eyes I had ever seen. The face that smiled at me was round and sunburnt, engraved with innumerable deep lines, but the body was stringy as gristle. 'Who's the memorial to?' I asked him as we shook hands. 'One of our great Boer generals,' he replied, and added simply: 'I'm his son, I look after the place.'

Thus I met, almost as in a reincarnation, one of the legendary Boer farmers of tradition. He gave me a packet of biltong, prepared by his wife ('the most beautiful woman in Africa'), and we sat in the back of his car and drank some lukewarm coffee out of a Thermos flask. He suffered from no false modesty ('I'm always giving, it's one of my failings') and he held violent and generally unshakeable opinions. Why, only a few days before he had sent a telegram to the Commonwealth Conference in London, warning the assembled leaders that communism, Catholicism and Jewry were secretly allied in a campaign to overthrow Western civilization. 'But they're blind, you know, *blind*. Churchill was just the same. I sent him a cable in 1942 – it cost me £7 – to warn him that Russia was anti-Christ, but he disregarded it. He never answered it at all. I suppose he read it?' said that old Boer, screwing up the Thermos flask. 'What do you think?'

So we chatted pleasantly, and he told me that if I ever came that way again I was welcome to stay at his farm and eat his biltong and disagree with his arguments for as long as I liked. It was a pleasure, said he, to meet a visitor from Britain, and that reminded him: had I seen the incontrovertible evidence at Bloemfontein concerning the ground glass and the porridge in British concentration camps during the Boer War?

Alien visitors

One evening I heard music in the street, and looking out of my window I saw two strange figures passing. One was a young man in a tall brown hat, blowing on a shepherd's flute. The other was attached by complex apparatus to a variety of apparently home-made instruments – bagpipes, drums, cymbals, a triangle I think – and in order to beat the biggest drum he had to move in an abrupt but creaky shuffle. Slowly and sporadically these engaging characters pottered down the pavement below me, tooling and drumming as they went. In Trieste that day they were like visitors from another, less inhibited world.

You're welcome

Here is an exchange I heard during an anti-American protest demonstration at Ottawa:

Police inspector: Are you a part of this demonstration,

which is forbidden as you know to go any closer to the
American embassy?

Protestor: No, sir, we are just Canadian citizens exercising
our right of free movement.

Inspector: Why are you carrying that placard, then?

Protestor: Oh, that's simply an expression of my own
personal views, as a Canadian citizen.

Inspector: I see. All right, go ahead, then.

Protestor: Thank you, sir.

Inspector: You're welcome.

I was in a stingy mood

In the ill-lit pedestrian tunnel that goes under the Elbe at
Dresden I heard ahead of me the strains of a Viennese waltz,
played by a pair of Gypsy violinists. I was in a stingy mood,
and resolved to give them nothing. As it happened there was
nobody else in the tunnel at that moment, and as I passed
the musicians, still eloquently playing, I felt their eyes
thoughtfully following me. I was decidedly self-conscious,
knowing very well that I ought to put something in the open
violin case at their feet, and as I walked towards the daylight
my resolution wavered. 'You should be ashamed of yourself,'
I said to myself, so when I emerged into the open I dug a few
coins out of my purse and re-entered the tunnel. Melodies
from the Vienna woods were still sounding in its twilight,
and the Gypsies were not in the least surprised to see me
back. They had read me like a book, and were expecting me.
I put my coins in their violin case, and they both bowed
courteously, without a smile. I bowed back in admiration.

Two Kiwis

Carefully and kindly the keeper placed the creature in my arms, and I felt its feathers rustling against my hands so sharp and metallic that they almost felt like scales. The beady little eyes were blind and filmed, the strong wire-like legs scratched and struggled against my chest, and the long tube of a beak, nostrils at the end of it, protruded its way crossly under my arm. It was about the size of a hen. The keeper looked on almost paternally.

Two Jocks

I watched an elderly man with sparse gingery hair strolling hands in pockets towards a pub on an Edinburgh corner, followed forty or fifty yards behind by his extremely aged collie dog. Sometimes the man looked round with an encouraging smile, and the dog smiled gamely back, and so they progressed in perfect rapport, like figures in a Burns poem, until the pair of them disappeared together into the malty shadows of the pub.

Four Londoners

I had an appointment with the pelicans of St James's Park, to whom each day a grateful Ministry of Works donates a ration of fish. Their keeper was waiting there with his bucket, and punctually at four o'clock a big white pelican waddled staidly out of the water and rubbed his beak ingratiatingly against the man's legs. 'This is Paul,' he said. 'He's a very good-natured bird.' Before long two others turned up, in rather a diffident, squint-eyed, lopsided manner, for they were newcomers to the park. 'They're funny birds, pelicans,' said the keeper. 'Some people like them, some don't.' But when he had fed them their fish, and they waddled away sated, he turned to me again. 'They've had enough, you see. They aren't greedy birds at all. I thought they behaved very well, didn't you? Very well indeed, considering.'

In academia

I have never forgotten the Christmas parties arranged for us, when I was a child, by the canons of Christ Church, Oxford, in their great canonical houses facing Tom Quad. How tall the candles were! How rich but wholesome the cakes! How twinkling the Regius professors turned out to be, stripped of the awful dignities of office! What thrilling presents we were given – envelopes with penny blacks upon them, magnificent wax seals of bishops or chancellors! How happy the old clergymen's faces looked as, breathlessly piping our gratitude – 'Thank you very much *indeed*, sir!' 'It was *jolly* nice of you, sir!' – we last saw them nodding their goodbyes, a little exhausted around the eyes, through the narrowing gaps of their front doors!

Definitely not

I was sitting upon a grassy incline in a park in Adelaide when two small boys, one rather smaller than the other, prepared to ride down the slope on their skateboards. There were a few beer bottles lying around, left over from the night before, and I heard the elder boy say to the younger, in an authoritative voice intended largely for my own ears: 'Please don't hit the lady – I don't mind about the beer bottles, but *definitely* not the lady.'

The captain of the *Saratoga*

The captain of the USS *Saratoga*, a tall lean man of ecclesiastical bearing, sits in a raised padded armchair on the port side of his bridge, rather as though he is having his hair cut or is being inducted to his see, and by looking through its tilted windows he can see the big jet bombers on the flight deck below. This ship, the publicity officer at your elbow tells you, has enough paint on her to redecorate 30,000 average American homes. There are 2,000 telephones on board, three escalators, three soda fountains, nine barbers' shops and 3,676 trouser hangers. 'We generate enough electricity to service a city the size of Pittsburgh, an industrial city in the State of Ohio. Our machines peel a thousand potatoes an hour.'

Below the windows the pilots scramble into their high cockpits. The captain rises from his chair, and a first violent roar of jet engines reverberates though the carrier. ('This ship has seventeen decks,' shouts the publicity officer indefatigably. 'There are more than 7,000 coffee cups on board the giant carrier, which is named from a battleground in the American Revolutionary War.') Then, suddenly, there screams into the corner of your eye a lean silver aircraft, violently projected at breakneck speed down the deck and into the blue, and in a moment there seem to be aircraft everywhere, some careering down the angled deck, some straight towards the bows, flashing and roaring and streaming away into the blue. In a moment or two the whole flight is gone, and is vanishing in the general direction of Turkey. A flash, a blast of jets, a dozen young men hurled brutally into the sky, and a terrible page of history could almost instantly be written. No wonder the captain of the *Saratoga*, as he returns to the seat of his command, has the air of a thoughtful but authoritative divine.

Young man with a gun

Up a dingy flight of stairs in Vienna I went to visit Dr Simon Wiesenthal, the Nazi hunter and himself a victim of the camps. Short, balding, in his seventies then, he was surrounded in his cluttered apartment by certificates of merit and scrolls of gratitude. He had devoted his later life to tracking down the last of the Nazi murderers and seeing that they were punished – year after year, decade after decade – while those once-swaggering SS men grew frail and forgetful, and Wiesenthal himself entered old age fired still by his merciless search for justice – or revenge. If he had anything to do with it, he told me, no single Nazi murderer, however old and grey, would ever be allowed to die in peace. I thought his office unforgettably baleful. The files that filled its walls were dreadful registers of death and torture, and Wiesenthal talked disturbingly about the wicked men still alive and flourishing in Europe. There had been an attempt on his life a few weeks before my visit, and a police guard had reluctantly been given him by the Viennese, whose communal conscience about the Jews was less than clear.

That day's sentry looked up at me as I left Wiesenthal's office. He was a blond long-haired youth with a gun on his lap, lounging there on a bench with his feet upon a chair, chewing something; and as he insolently stared at me, and at the old gentleman saying goodbye to me at the door, I felt an uneasy frisson.

More organic patriots

Being myself a sort of self-adopted Swiss patriot, I made a pilgrimage once to the lakeside field of Rütli, which is the traditional birthplace of the Swiss nation. On the Sunday I walked down the track from the heights above, thousands of more organic patriots were making their way to or from the hallowed site, most of them evidently people from the mountain country around. I offered a cheerful good morning to everyone I met, and could not help admiring the utter lack of ingratiation, the courtesy tinged with decidedly suspended and unsmiling judgement, with which most of them responded. I was struck too by the proportion of twisted, stooped or withered old people among them – people of a kind that had almost vanished from the rest of western Europe. They were one generation removed from the goitre, that talismanic affliction of mountain peasantries, and the faces of those crooked ancients – hard hewn, bashed about, gaunt – seemed to speak of centuries of earthy hardship, isolation and suspicion. I could not help remembering, too, that in Switzerland the very last European witch was publicly burnt.

Fishing lady

On the edge of a swamp in Louisiana an old Negro woman in a floppy straw hat was fishing in the oozy water with a home-cut rod. She had already caught a few fish, and they were floundering in the shallows, tied up in a net. She told me she had been dropped there that morning from the train which passed nearby; her husband worked on the railroads, and in the evening, when the train came back again, it would slow down past the swamp and allow her to scramble aboard a freight car. She asked me to drive a little way down the road and fetch her some Coca-Cola. I bought her four bottles, and the last I saw of her she was standing on the boggy bank in her huge hat, with the rod in one hand and a bottle raised to her lips with the other, a portly statuesque figure against a gloomy background of cypress trees.

Coffee time

I was once standing at the entrance to the celebrated whores' alley of Hamburg, beneath the flickering neon sky of the Reeperbahn, when an unexpected figure passed through its portals, weaving a bustling, purposeful, businesslike way among the pallid lechers loitering inside. It was a waiter from a neighbouring cafe, nattily dressed in white and carrying a cup of coffee neatly on his polished tray, with two lumps of sugar hygienically wrapped. He made his way dexterously to one of the brothel windows and, peering into the gloom to pick his customer from the row of ghoul-like prostitutes inside – dim, apparently phosphorescent images of flesh, paint and pink nylon – he handed her the tray with a polite little bow and returned to the world outside.

In London, 1980s

Somewhere in Oxford Street, towards the end of the afternoon, a sort of hallucination seemed to overcome me, and I found myself in a nightmare limbo. I was aghast. Who were these fearful people, of no particular race, of no particular kind, so crude and elvish of face, so shambling of gait, so shabby of clothes, so degraded and demeaned of bearing? Where were they shoving and sidling their way to? What culture did they represent, what traditions inspired them, what loyalty did they cherish, what God did they worship? I seriously doubt if a less prepossessing citizenry can be found anywhere on earth than the citizenry frequenting such streets of London.

Magnifique!

When I was dining one night in a restaurant in the French island of Martinique, an extraordinary girl burst into the dining room and began dancing a kind of ferocious screeching rumba. She wore an enormous tricorn hat and a red swimsuit, and when the management objected to her presence she instantly threw herself into a spectacularly flamboyant tantrum. She screamed, shouted, sang ear-splitting snatches of songs, threw plates about, dropped her hat, made savage faces at the customers, knocked tables over and reduced the whole room to helpless laughter until at last, to crown a splendid entertainment, somebody dialled the wrong number and obtained, instead of the police, the fire brigade, whose clanking red engines skidded to a halt outside our windows and whose helmeted officers, trailing axes and hoses, stared in bewilderment through the open doors at the hilarious chaos inside. 'It was magnificent!' was the general verdict as, wiping our eyes and resuming our victuals, we watched that uninhibited performer withdraw.

West Pointer

It was Saturday afternoon at West Point, and many of the cadets were preparing to go out. I saw one emerging from her barracks in what I took to be her semi-dress uniform – a trim grey trouser suit with a shiny peaked cap, very smart and flattering to her lithe figure. I followed her down the path towards the Eisenhower statue – left right, left right, head up, arms swinging, brisk as could be to where her father was waiting to greet her: and then, talk about symbolisms! He was your very image of a kindly homespun countryman, a figure from an old magazine cover, wearing boots and a floppy brown hat, his face shining with pride and happiness. She broke into a run, her cap went askew for a moment, and into his strong American arms she fell.

An Irish experience

I was in Dublin for the first time in my life, and I took a stroll along the extended breakwater, bleached in sun and sea wind, that protects the mouth of the Liffey from the exuberance of the Irish Sea. Gazing about me pleasurably, presently I saw implanted across the causeway the clubhouse of the Half Moon Swimming Club, and immediately beside the door of the building there was a bench, facing directly down the mole, as though in judgement. Even from a distance I could see that four or five heavy pinkish figure occupied this seat, motionless but glistening in the sun, like Buddhas, and I could feel their eyes steadily focused upon me as I approached them down the causeway until at last, reaching the purlieus of the club, I raised my own eyes modestly to meet those divinities face to face. Five old, fat, gleaming Dubliners looked back at me severely, and they were all entirely nude.

Young Iceland

Children play a disproportionate part in Icelandic life, it seems to me. Nothing is more surprising than to hand over one's fare in a country bus and find it accepted by a character apparently not much more than four years old, who grumbles with absolute adult authenticity if you haven't got the right change. And in the Althing, the Icelandic parliament, a common sight is a minuscule page hastening in with a quotation for the Foreign Minister, perhaps, or a statistic for the Minister of Finance: he is likely to be wearing a check shirt, a green jersey and corduroy trousers, and as often as not he interrupts the flow of debate by banging the door behind him. Nobody minds. Drat the boy, one seems to hear them murmuring. And his father was just the same.

After Perón

General Perón's dictatorship of Argentina had ended, but in the plush *fin-de-siècle* cafe I chose for my lunch in Buenos Aires his presence was still palpable. Around me gaggles of elderly women were sipping Cinzano with soda water and nibbling biscuits, nuts and bits of flabby cheese, but in the dimmer recesses of the room various lonely men were deep in the contemplation of *La Prensa*. When I asked my waiter if there were still many Peronistas about he nodded darkly but wryly, with a flicker of his thumb, towards those several grey solitaries in the corners, who certainly had a brooding conspiratorial look to them but were probably, in fact, looking through the small advertisements for second-hand canoes.

The proclamation

A stone's throw from the holiday madhouses of Waikiki there stands a row of rickety tables beside the sea, shaded by straw matting, where elderly Honolulu citizens while away their Sunday mornings with chess, chequers and inexplicable card games. I was sitting there in reverie one morning, happily lost in the sun and the salt breezes, when a prickly old gentleman on the benches beside me touched me on the shoulder. 'You look a little melancholy,' he said kindly. 'Aintcha read the proclamation?' – and he pointed to the notice painted on a weatherboard above us. 'This is a Public Park,' it said. 'Have Fun!'

Reassurance

I was in the Isle of Man for the first time in my life, to write an essay about it. I had bought a book about Manx folklore and, finding an open-air cafe beside the sea, settled down to read it with a plate of prawns and a Guinness. The sun was lovely, the prawns were excellent, the Guinness went down like a treat, and I congratulated myself upon my choice of profession. Presently a lady came over to my table and handed me a pamphlet. 'Oh, thank you,' I said, 'how kind of you. What's it about?' 'Oh my dear,' she emolliently replied, 'it is only to reassure you that God is always with the lonely.'

No reply

Nowhere on earth is so inexorably improving as Washington, DC. When we came down from the top of the Washington Monument even the elevator operator dismissed us with a parting injunction. 'Let's all work,' he said, 'to clean up our country for the two-hundredth anniversary just coming up.'

'Yes sir,' we dutifully replied, 'you're darned right – you hear that, kids?'

He had not, however, finished yet. 'And I'm talking,' he darkly added, 'about the mental aspects as well as the physical.'

We had no answer to that.

Possibilities of misfortune

The Kashmiris are a hospitable people, but not inspiriting. They seem to be considering always the possibilities of misfortune. In the autumn the fall of the leaf seems a personal affliction to them, and the passing of the year depresses them like the fading of their own powers. Then in the chill evenings the women disappear into their private quarters, and the men light their little baskets of charcoal, tuck them under their fustian cloaks and squat morosely in the twilight, their unshaven faces displaying a faint but telling disquiet. There was a touching pathos, I thought, to their style. 'How do you like your life?' I asked one new acquaintance there, when we had progressed into intimacy. 'Excellent,' he replied with a look of inexpressible regret. 'I love every minute of it' – and he withdrew a cold hand from the recesses of his cloak, and waved it listlessly in the air to illustrate his enjoyment.

My dinner companion

Marvellously lithe and light-footed are the people of Helsinki, big but agile, jovial at smorgasbords or loping across their snowfields like Tibetan holy men. Their children, slithering about with hockey sticks, give the heartening impression that they came into the world on skis. Their wives are neat as pins, and gossip sharply in expensive coffee shops. They are a people that nobody in the world could possibly be sorry for. They are sharp as nails, and twice as spiky. But here's an odd and provoking fact. When I wanted something to read with my dinner some unexpected instinct guided my choice, a kind of reluctant nostalgia, a niggling trace of respect and affection, and when I sat down to my pig's trotters I found myself dining with Turgenev: and all that brave and courteous citizenry, I felt, could not offer me quite such company.

Diplomats and a pianist

I once went to the British embassy in Washington, DC, to see the pianist Vladimir Horowitz presented with the Gold Medal of the Royal Philharmonic Society, brought to him on a cushion by a marvellously suave young secretary and handed over with a graceful ambassadorial speech about violent times and the meaning of art. Mr Horowitz seemed pleased, but instead of replying in kind sat down at the piano and played in a highly vibrant and indeed imperial manner 'God Save the Queen', making full use of the sustaining pedal.

There was a pause at the end of it, and instantly, as the last notes faded, I clicked the scene in my memory: and so I have held it there like a flash from a dream, the ambassador benignly at attention, the young diplomats rigid all about, the American guests clutching their champagne glasses, the great room aglow with carpets and portraits, the pianist's hand raised in a last grandiloquence – an ornate little vignette of Washington, where life so often shimmers through a gauze curtain, insubstantially.

Impact!

King Sobhuza of Swaziland, one of the world's last absolute monarchs, offered me a kindly greeting. His subjects fell on their knees, or even on their faces, when he passed, but I looked him Jeffersonianly in the eye, and shall never forget the moment. He had the most remarkable, most twinkling, most mischievous, altogether most entertaining face in the world. He seemed to radiate an amused but resolute complicity, as though he knew what a charade life was but was determined to make the most of it. He was dressed that day in European clothes; when he wore his tribal costume, a stunning assembly of feathers, bright textiles and talismanic brooches, the effect must have been terrific.

Style

I joined an eminent, kind and cultivated actress in taking a cab to an address on Second Avenue in Manhattan. Said the cab driver: 'Whereabouts is that on Second Avenue, lady?' Without a flicker in her elegant equanimity she replied: 'Don't ask me, bud. You're the fucking cab driver.'

On an Oxford evening

Loitering around Magdalen College on a classic May evening I saw a company of players making their way through the trees for a performance of *A Midsummer Night's Dream*. They were moving swiftly in their cowls, ruffs and velvets, all among the elms, and a few shy deer watched them pass between the tree trunks. Their footfalls were silent on the turf, their voices reached me faintly on the warm air, and they disappeared into the shadows merrily, with Puck occasionally practising his jumps, and Titania lifting her crimson skirts, and a few lumpish fairies skirmishing in the flanks. I never caught the spell of the theatre more hauntingly, as I watched them across the fence, and felt like Hamlet when the players came to Elsinore – 'You are welcome, masters, welcome all.'

The moment of victory

An old woman, horribly crippled, struggles down the last few steps of the Chapel of St Helena, in the Church of the Holy Sepulchre at Jerusalem. It is a faintly illuminated crypt. Her progress is agonizingly slow, but she is determined to reach the altar by herself. Painfully with her two sticks she shuffles down the stone steps, each one a torment. Prayers are mingled with her breathing. When at least she reaches the bottom, though, and I peer into the darkness to watch her, she abruptly leans down and places her sticks beside her on the ground. Then, straightening herself as far as her old crooked frame will allow her, she raises her arms above her in triumph and exuberance, more like some whipcord young athlete at the moment of victory than a poor old woman, distorted and arthritic, who would soon have to face the steps again.

At Schwab's

Hardly a Hollywood memoir is complete without a reference to Schwab's, 'The World's Most Famous Drugstore', and it is still heavy with the old mystique. Elderly widows of émigré directors reminisce about Prague over their breakfasts. Young men in jerkins and expensive shoes ostentatiously read *Variety*, or greet each other with stagey endearments. Ever and again one hears exchanges of critiques across the hubbub – 'I love her, she's a fine, fine actress, but it just wasn't *her* . . .' – 'Well, but what can one expect with Philip directing, she needs *definite* direction' – 'True, but shit, it just made me *puke*, the way she did that last scene . . .' I took to sharing a table with the divorced wife of a Mexican set designer who shared my enthusiasm for Abyssinian cats.

A royal court

I had an introduction to a Mogul princess, of the dynasty which made Delhi its capital in the seventeenth century and built the very walled city in whose labyrinthine recesses she lives. I found her ensconced in her front sitting room between portraits of her imperial forebears: a short, decisive old lady with a brief mischievous smile and an air of totally liberated self-possession. Her antique mansion is a beguiling shambles in the old Islamic style: a couple of rooms in the Western manner for the convenience of visitors, the rest more or less medieval – wide decrepit courtyard, dusty trellised vine, thickly populated chambers all around. There are granddaughters and sons-in-law and undefined connections; there are skivvies and laundrymen and assorted sweepers; there are children and dogs and unexplained loiterers in doorways. Forty or fifty souls constitute the tumbled court of the Begum Timur Jehan, and through it she moves commandingly in green trousers, issuing instructions, reminiscing about emperors, traitors or ladies of the harem, and frequently consulting her highly organized notebook, all asterisks and cross-references, for addresses or reminders.

Politicians

⟿

I love to watch the politicians ushering their constituents around the Capitol in Washington, DC, benign and avuncular, and to observe the endearing combination of the condescending and the wheedling with which they shake hands with their respectful electors at the end of the tour – 'We sure are obliged to you, Congressman' – 'We certainly are, sir' – 'I shall never forget this day, Congressman' – '*Fine, fine, great to have you along . . .*' Meeting a likely looking gent in a Capitol corridor, I tried a gambit myself, as a speculation. 'Morning, Senator,' I said. 'Hullo there, young lady,' he instantly replied. 'Having fun?' – and off he strode to his office, chomping, alas for my purposes, not an actual, but at least a metaphorical cigar.

Perfect understanding

Long after the end of the British Empire, some of its manners balefully survived. In Patna I had occasion to go to the Secretariat to ask permission to take photographs of the city, and found myself before a functionary of such classic insolence, such an unassailable mixture of resentment, patronage, self-satisfaction and effrontery that for a moment I felt like picking up his inkwell and throwing it at him. But I bit my lip and restrained myself, and as I glared back at him there the scales dropped from my eyes: his image blurred and reassembled before me, his colour paled somewhat, and I saw before me his true archetype and inspiration, the lesser English civil servant – now, as in imperial times, the insufferable master of his art. I thanked the man profusely and assured him that I understood *perfectly* why I would have to make an application in triplicate to the Divisional Officer, who would unfortunately not be on duty until the following Wednesday afternoon.

Snow in Holland

I was once in Amsterdam when the first snow of the winter fell. The men in the central junk market, among their stuffed birds and rusty curios from Surinam, broke up the most hopelessly lopsided of their kitchen chairs and made bonfires of them. A cold wind whistled in from the North Sea, huddling the more mature housewives in their mutation minks and driving the portly burghers to the felt-covered newspaper tables of the cafes, where they meditated ponderously over their coffees like so many East India merchants considering the price of apes.

Joburgers

I found the poor black inhabitants of the Johannesburg locations, in the cruel days of apartheid, hard to understand. Sometimes they were grave and courteous, and I was reminded of Ethiopian chieftains; sometimes they treated me with such bubbling flippancy that I thought they might be teasing me; sometimes a flash of malice entered their eyes, or something gave them such inexplicable amusement that they burst into a tumult of infectious laughter, or danced little jazzy jigs upon the pavement. When they spoke, they did so with explosive animation, but when they listened the whole of their being supplemented their hearing, they became one great ear, and their white eyes, their tense bodies, their eager fingers and their yellow striped socks all waited upon my words. And once in my hotel I heard tinny twangs of music from the street outside; and there beneath the arcades of President Street a solitary black man was lounging by, in a crumpled brown hat and blue dungarees, plucking away at a guitar as he walked, humming a high-toned melody, and expressing in his every gesture, in the very swing of his shoulders, the spirit of blithe indolence.

'The same again'

Kabul in the 1960s is a tense, nervous, shifty capital, and edgiest of all at night, when the streetlights are dimmed, the brilliant Asian stars come up above the hills and only a few shrouded watchmen are left brooding on the doorsteps. Then the whole place feels sleepless and dry-eyed, like some insomniac conspirator. Sometimes a shot rings dead on the night, and sometimes a distant shout, and when a donkey pads softly by you can hear the two men upon its back, neb-ulous in white robes, murmuring to each other in low spor-adic undertones. I once asked an old man of Kabul what would happen if another enemy attacked this capital as the British had catastrophically attacked it in 1845. Would they be exterminated too? He gave an angry tug at his beard and threw me a look of piercing and bloodshot intensity. 'The same,' he hissed through the last of his teeth. 'The same again!'

Home are the hunters!

I first went to Kuwait in the company of a sheikhly hawking party, returning home from a desert sporting expedition. Splendid were the caparisons of those haughty Arabian sportsmen, and their eyes were cold and heavy-lidded. They wore magnificent flowered gowns, and crossed bandoliers, and daggers, and spotless headdresses, and golden swords; and big black lackeys carried their peregrine falcons, hooded upon their pedestals; and a brass band puffed away on the airfield at Kuwait when this gorgeous crew, looking slightly airsick, staggered on to the ancestral soil.

The quarry clerk

I was only just in time to meet Bob Owen of Croesor, in northern Wales, before he died in 1962, and I am glad I didn't miss him. He had worked as a clerk for a local quarry company for more than thirty years, a small man with a high wrinkled brow, a white moustache and bushy eyebrows, respectably dressed when I met him in jacket, waistcoat and unassertive tie. He was a tremendous talker, a chain smoker and a chapel goer of strong views, and when his quarry work ended he had become a writer and lecturer well known throughout Wales. He took me to the small square house where he and his wife lived and, merciful heavens, the moment he opened the front door for me I found myself hemmed in, towered over, squashed in, squeezed down by an almighty multitude of books. They filled every room of the house – he had amassed more than 40,000 books and pamphlets, many of them rare and valuable. He was born, he told me, in a very small nearby cottage, nicknamed Twll Wenci, and people used to call him Bob Twll Wenci – Bob Weasel's Hole.

Pretty children

In the mountain resort of Flims I saw three small Swiss girls on their way home from school. They looked like modernistic elves, with bright-coloured rucksacks on their backs, and they were burbling brightly to each other as they climbed the hill to their homes above the town. They paused for a bit of gossip and leg-swinging at a bench beside the road, and when they got up to go one of them, meandering off by herself, chanced to leave her sunglasses on the bench. In a trice the other two, laughing and giggling, threw them on the ground and stamped them into pieces before my eyes, alternating kicks in the prettiest way.

Lese-majesty

'Yeah,' said a woman loudly and complacently, stepping back from a china cabinet during our guided tour of the White House. 'Just what I thought – *chipped!*'

A hated man

Soon after World War II a friend was driving me one day along an Oxfordshire lane when we saw a picturesque sight in front of us. A fine four-in-hand was running along at a spanking pace, driven by an elderly gentlemanly looking coachman on his high box. 'D'you see the man driving it?' said my host. 'That's Air Marshal Sir Arthur Harris, the most hated Englishman alive.'

'Bomber' Harris! The man who had unleashed his vast fleets of thudding black aircraft, manned by crews from every corner of the old British Empire, to devastate half Germany and kill scores of thousands of German civilians! I stared rudely at him through our rear window, as we left those trotting horses behind, but he looked a jolly enough old fellow, up there behind the reins.

America, America!

I once came into Pier 86 on the liner *United States*, the fastest ever built, and I watched the faces of the passengers around me, waiting for the gangplank to open as the ship's band subsided into a last medley of patriotism – 'America, America', 'Dixie', 'Star-Spangled Banner' and one or two stirring marches I failed to recognize. Trilly secretarial voices rang, as those grand old tunes reverberated, jewelled spectacles vibrated, stiletto heels tapped the deck; but the expressions on the passengers' faces struck me as sad, as though the hum of the liner's mechanisms, the blaring of those anthems as the vessel docked, were holding the voyagers for a moment in a lost American world – a world encapsulated there still between the decks of the great ship, that would dissipate the moment the gangplank doors were opened, and they returned to 46th Street.

Responses on the road

⁓

Driving through Vienna in a rented car, I slowed down uncertainly to decide upon my route. Instantly the driver in the car behind blasted his horn most rudely. I gave him a vulgar two-fingered sign which I would never have dreamed of using had I not recently learnt that it was a gesture devised by Welsh archers to demonstrate to opponents that their shooting fingers were intact. When the other car overtook me, its occupants both looked eagerly in my direction. The stout tight-buttoned horn-rimmed burgher at the wheel shook his jowls at me in affronted astonishment. His wife blew me a kiss.

Widowhood

⁓

For the jollier kind of American widow Los Angeles offers a cheerful refuge, and provides a bedrock, so to speak, upon which they can reconstruct their lives. There is a certain sameness to their appearance, in their bright blouses, leather jerkins, rather too tight slacks and rather too rakish sailor caps. They are bowed often with arthritis but resolutely jaunty of step, and to their attitudes there is a sprightly element of freedom. 'Did you know,' one such lady asked me, supposing me, I imagine, to be a bit lost for social satisfactions, 'did you know that the telephone company offers a free tour every day of the week? My, that's a rewarding way of spending an afternoon!'

Moon men

In the last years of Rhodesia, before it mutated into Zimbabwe, I sometimes had the feeling that its Europeans were being mutated by history, becoming some sort of new subspecies as they fruitlessly resisted the rise of black power. In Salisbury I sometimes took my lunch beside the hotel pool, and there was generally a group of young officers, on leave from their battle stations in the bush, having a swim or a beer on the terrace. Stripped to their trunks and sun-bleached hair, they seemed to lose all ethnic identity. Some were probably mercenaries: Portuguese, German, Afrikaner; most were doubtless expatriate Britons, subtly changed in posture and physique; all seemed to me specific not simply to the place, but to the time, to the circumstances, the historical prospect. They might have been moon men.

Ethel in Egypt

One evening I went to a salon presided over by one of the younger, richer and more cosmopolitan of the Cairo society ladies. The purpose was to present to the Cairo *grand monde* a celebrated clairvoyant of indeterminate Levantine origin, named – well, let us say Ethel. Ethel would judge character, tell fortunes, give semi-occult advice and accept confidences. The attendance was soignée: a couple of ambassadors' wives, an Indian, a German, a few bangled Egyptian patricians. We were served coffee in very fragile cups, by a Berber in a tarboosh, and we sat on squashy sofas at spindly tables in a room above the Nile.

Ethel was closeted on a balcony, and one by one the guests disappeared for consultations, taking their coffee cups with them. In the meantime the rest of us chatted. Did we know that G was almost certainly going to St Tropez with A? Was it really true that B was getting Omani money for his new hotel? Had we tried the chopped liver at the Hilton? What about F selling that awful house of his for a quarter of a million?

From time to time another woman left for the confessional, but the returning devotees, I noticed, never seemed dismayed by Ethel's predictions, and returned instantly, without so much as a mention of their brush with the occult, to our distinctly worldly exchange – '*Half a million, I heard – and surely it's chopped kidneys? . . .*' But then Ethel, my hostess told me, seldom had unhappy premonitions. 'Well, one would hardly expect her to, would one, actually in one's own drawing room?'

Birth of a taste

I had disliked whisky all my life, but stopping to eat my corned beef sandwich in one of the most famous Scottish distillery areas, I felt it my duty to try once more. I went to a nearby pub and asked for a dram of the local water of life, to drink with my victuals on a bench in the square outside. The barmaid looked at me quizzically. 'I'm not sure the law allows it, but seeing as you're a visitor . . .' Looking cautiously around her, she poured into my plastic mug a full measure of single malt whisky – one of the very best, she said, from a distillery just down the road. I concealed it in my bag as I left the inn, and turning at the door I saw her winking at me conspiratorially, as if I had poached a salmon. No constable intervened, though. No revenue man expostulated. Unwrapping my sandwich, there on the bench in the square I took a cautious swig of the whisky, and, dear God, I have never looked back.

Hospitable cop

I was a guest once at a Buckingham Palace reception for publishers and writers, and at the end of the evening, wishing to leave, I looked around for somebody to thank. Queen, princes, dukes and all seemed to have gone elsewhere, so I left anyway, and at the palace gates I found a policeman. 'I was brought up,' I told him, 'to say thank you for having me when I'd been to a party, so as I can't find the Queen or anybody to say it to, I'll say it to you instead. Thank you very much for having me.'

'Not at all, madam,' he replied. 'Come again.'

A glimpse of power, 1950s

For a glimpse of power, try the Bolshoi at Moscow, when some gigantic Russian epic is being furiously enacted, with rolls of kettle drums and clashes of armour, a mammoth chorus open-mouthed, a clutch of heroes swelling in the foreground, with a passage and repassage of knights, horses, serfs, a frenzy of conical helmets and chain mail, banners dramatically waving, flames issuing from a backcloth, smoke, flashing beacons, the orchestra in a quivering fortissimo, the conductor wiping his sweating bald head, the enormous audience gripping its seats or craning from the high gilded balconies above the chandelier – then, in the middle of it all, you will glance across your neighbour's shoulder to the great state box in the centre: and there will be sitting the most powerful man on earth, looking bored and rather glazed, a slight sad smile playing around the corners of his mouth, his wife, in a bun and brown sagging dress, demure and attentive at his elbow. You need not wait for the last act. Go home and sleep it off.

Another time, perhaps

In the Faroe Islands I repeatedly ran into groups of traditionally dressed folk persons, buckled and aproned, on their way to or from festivals of one kind or another. 'We have been telling rhymes in Klaksvik,' one practitioner told me as we sat together on the deck of a ferry, a celestial scene of mountain and fjord streaming by. 'Long rhymes?' I ventured to ask, thinking I might be fortunate to have missed them. '*Extremely* long,' he said with pride.

At a Patagonian airfield

When I was once hanging about an airfield in Patagonia, hoping to arrange a lift to the north, I noticed a small group of people, dressed apparently for après-ski, who seemed to dominate the waiting room with a kind of steely radiance.

They looked very rich and very brassy and very thrusting. Their children were ill mannered but intensely vivacious, their women were gimlet eyed but seductive, their men had a feline Italian elegance to them; and unexpectedly, when I offered a smile in their direction, one and all suddenly, brilliantly, delightfully smiled back. I asked where these magical creatures were making for, and was answered in one short tingling word: 'Rio!'

Makings of a microcosm

I did not want to be rude, but I could not help eyeing my neighbour with interest, for she seemed to me to have the makings of a microcosm. More than most cities, Stockholm projects two images – the one you have been led to expect and the one you discover for yourself – and this plump but not unalluring citizen, wearing a pink linen dress and a white straw hat, her eyes bluish but somehow glazed, her mastication rhythmic and her bosom calmly heaving to the flow of the salad – this lady of Stockholm, evocative partly of Chanel and partly of disinfectant, slipped into my preconceptions like a plug into a socket. She was eating alone, with a half bottle of Niersteiner and what appeared to be the financial page of *Svenska Dagbladet*. Her lunch was large but looked obscurely colourless, as though it had been bleached in some anti-fattening lotion. Her gaze now and then wandered from her victuals and paraded slowly, resting at last without excitement on somebody else's pudding. Her expression was content without being joyous, and beneath her loose blonde curls, I told myself, all kinds of Swedish neuroses surely festered: anxieties of opulence, spinsterhood or free love, occupational frustrations and suicidal impulses. She seemed to express all that I expected of Stockholm, and when at last I engaged her in conversation, and boldly asked her what she did for a living, I could almost have hugged her in gratitude. 'I am a juvenile social welfare worker,' she replied with a sweet smile, taking a delicate last sip of the hock.

The only place for him

When the US Supreme Court ended racial segregation in American schools, all the simmering discontent of the white Southerners boiled over, and I spent the day in Atlanta listening to angry men and women. The abuse they used was at once so theatrical and so repetitive that I could scarcely believe it had not been plucked wholesale from some common phrasebook of prejudice. I joined a conversation, in a coffee shop, with the manager of the place and a man who told me he was a senior police officer. They spend some time reminiscing about race riots of the past, talking comfortably of niggers bashed and beaten in the streets; and of one especially, hounded by the mob, who had thrown himself into the doorway of that very coffee shop, only to be pushed back on to the pavement. 'The only place for a nigger,' said the manager with finality, 'is at the back door, with his hat in his hand.'

Flowers and the tribesmen

Clumps of a rhododendron-like bush brightened the fresh meadows as we drove through the Qara tribal country of south-east Arabia, and I asked the Arab driver to stop while I jumped out of the truck to pick some blossoms.

'What do you want them for?' he asked when I returned with the flowers. 'Are they good for diseases?'

'I don't think so. I just thought they looked nice.'

'So they do, so they do. But the Qara people eat them, for the stomach.'

'Are you *sure?*'

'Quite sure. The Qara people know everything about flowers and things. They are very strange people, like the animals. By Allah! They are very like the animals.'

As if to bear him out we saw at that moment three strange fuzzy tribesmen standing on a bank beside the road, leather thongs around their foreheads, dark robes slung over their shoulders, daggers at their belts. My driver shouted them a ribald greeting. Two of them, with long, beautiful faces, did not respond, but simply stood there stiffly, like childish elocutionists waiting to perform; the third, a younger man, ventured to wave his short stick at us, and then, seeing that his companions remained impassive, lowered it shamefacedly as though guilty of some desperate solecism.

When we had passed I leant out of the window to look back at them. There they were still, three straight, shy figures, holding their sticks, watching our progress fixedly.

Uncle Henry and the planter

The planter, fresh from a tussle with his tractor, had greasy hands and wore a toupee and an open-necked shirt. But like most Southern gentlemen he had a talent for hospitality, and soon we were sitting on the balustrade of his porch, sipping long cool drinks and looking out through the pines. The plantation had once extended to some 10,000 acres of cotton, tobacco, sweet potatoes and corn, but was now whittled down to about 150 acres. He told me that he ran it with only one full-time employee. His children went to the local state school, his wife did the housework, and 'The Street', the double row of uniform cottages where the slaves used to live, was empty and tumbledown.

While we were talking on the porch a great cloud of dust approached us from the drive, and there emerged in stately motion two large mules. They were pulling a kind of sledge, a cross between a bobsled and Cleopatra's barge, and sitting on it, very old and dignified, was a Negro in a straw hat. Round the corner he came in imperial state, the mules panting, the sledge creaking, the dust billowing around us, and as he passed the porch he raised his hat by its crown and called: 'G'd evening, boss, sir; g'd evening, Missus Parker.' 'Good evening, Uncle Henry,' they replied.

He was an old retainer of the Parkers who lived almost entirely on their kindness. He was given a house and a few acres, firewood and storage space and a loan when he needed one. The planter would not see him in distress for the world. But to suggest that he might invite the old man into his house, or even shake hands with him, would be more than an impertinence, but might well be construed as a deliberate insult. Uncle Henry will always have a home, but, after all, the race must be preserved.

Family home

~~~

After a while I felt quite familiar with the social·structure of St Andrew's, New Brunswick. Who was this, for instance, smiling at me so kindly from the Wren House on Queen Street? Why, who but Miss Lelia Wren, who lives with her sister Miss Frances in the house their family has occupied for 150 years. Who is at the helm of that white boat out there? Mr Hered Hatt the scallop fisherman, of course – everyone knows that. In no time at all I was acquainted with Mr Ian Mackay, who owns the Shiretown Inn, and with Mrs Bobby Cockburn, whose late husband's pharmacy was one of the town's prime power centres, and very soon the Venerable Nantlais Jones was waving to me from his handsome Buick Park Avenue limousine, which has CLERGY in ecclesiastical lettering on its windscreen. Hardly has one well-known householder introduced me to her stately collection of teddy bears ('That's Boogy, that's Oogy, that's Daddy Bear in the corner') before another is telling me how effective birth control pills have proved in the propagation of her hibiscus plants.

It was like exploring a rambling old family home, the streets its corridors, the houses its rooms, the citizens its extremely gossipy owners and retainers. One morning I arranged to meet two of the town's many widows and, idly passing the time beforehand by wandering through the town cemetery, I found both those ladies' names already inscribed upon gravestones, below their departed husbands'.

Key West, 1960s

～

Key West is full of people with nothing much to do, but a talent for lounging gracefully in doorways. If I stood on the waterfront on a sunny morning I would soon find other idlers wandering to my side to stare at the water with me, and sometimes gentlemen would buttonhole me with dark questions. Was I looking for rare fish? Had I spoken to Mr Alvark? Was it right, what the papers were saying about convertibility? Did I realize that the deputation from Ecuador was arriving next day? What did the British government think about labour restrictions in Peru? Most of them had wild gleams in their eyes, and having said their queer bit, shuffled away like disappointed saboteurs. Slow and old is the island city of Key West; also surreptitious, bland and turtle-like.

All in the family

～

At the railway station at Assiut an elderly Copt had come to meet me. We sat in the station cafe for a preliminary cup of coffee, and he undid the buttons of his tight linen jacket and wiped his head fastidiously with a silk handkerchief. 'I come from a family of priests,' he said by way of introduction. 'There have been Christian priests in my family since AD 48, when St Mark paid his visit to Assiut; and before that my family, through unnumbered centuries, provided priestly acolytes for the local god of Assiut, Leci. Come, finish your coffee while I settle this infamous account.'

Marching with us!

One evening we were driving down a road on the outskirts of Chattanooga when we saw a dirty marquee. From it there came strains of music, with accompanying desultory snatches of women's voices, so we stopped at once and went inside. At the end of the tent a very fat woman was lying on the ground quivering and shaking, sometimes tremulously, like a jelly, sometimes with sharp stabs of impulsive movement. Two fierce women were supporting her head, and standing above them, waving his arms like a Paganini, prancing crazily here and there, a youth was strumming on a guitar. In the background a small girl was banging a hymn tune on an upright piano, and a group of black ladies, respectably dressed, looking a trifle bored, and sometimes pausing to exchange gossip or look out of the tent flap, was half-heartedly singing some sacred words: 'I'll never go hungry or know poverty/ So long as the good Lord is marching with me./ Marching with me! Marching with thee!/ So long as the good Lord is marching with me.'

Presently the prostrate patient, with heavings and convulsions, tried to gasp a few words, and at this the attendant harpies were galvanized. Seizing the patient by the front of her dress, they yanked her into a sitting position and hissed urgent instructions into her ear. She was still jerking incessantly. 'Take Him in, take Him in!' they hissed, and were soon screaming, 'Take Him in! Roll it! O Jesus, the glory of it!' until the patient herself, jerking and jumping, managed to croak from her constricted throat a few unintelligible syllables.

When we left the marquee she was still unhealed. The

guitarist still whirled about her. The piano still tinnily clanged. The lady choristers whined their listless hymn. And the convulsed patient, all her draperies loose by now, was still being urged to 'Let Him in, sister! Glory, glory, roll it, roll it!' by the demon women at her side.

Economic imperative

In the worst times of the Irish troubles, when Belfast was more or less in a state of war, I once saw a patrol of five or six British infantrymen moving cautiously and watchfully through the city centre in the prescribed mode – guns cocked, helmeted heads constantly turning right and left, lead man well in front, rearguard walking backwards with his finger on the trigger. As they passed an office of the National Westminster Bank one of them peeled away, while the others crouched there covering his back, ready for instant fire. He put his card in the bank's cash dispenser, he tucked his money away in a pocket of his camouflage suit, and they proceeded grimly on their prowl.

Sporting pleasures!

My first floodlit cricket match, in Sydney, was a terrific affair. Australia were playing New Zealand, and passions ran high. If a wicket fell or a catch was missed the crowd burst into magnificent displays of emotion, throwing hats, paper, cups and balloons into the air, shouting, whistling, clapping, booing and cheering. I was exhilarated! In the course of the game I happened to look over the balcony into an open space outside the stadium, and there I saw a succession of young men being hauled in, handcuffed by plainclothes policemen, briskly questioned, photographed there and then and shoved into a windowless van from whose interior emerged muffled thumps of protest. A few yards away, within sight of the police but on the safe side of a high wire-mesh fence, three small boys were getting their own kicks by sniffing aerosol cans.

The French swimmer

To my right, as I sat beside the harbour at La Rochelle, there came into my field of view a swimming man. He was in his fifties, I would guess, but stout and muscular, and he was swimming with an absolute rhythmic exactitude. A slow and powerful crawl, one two, one two, deep wallowing in the water went his head, up came his podgy arm, out emerged his face for breath, running with salt water – a slight pause at the top of his stroke, and he was down again half submerged. He never wavered. The pace of his stroke was metronomic, and it suddenly occurred to me that he was on the way somewhere, as one might walk to work, or take a bus. He was the first swimmer I ever saw who was using his crawl as a means of transport. I watched him intently, and once I thought I caught his eye, as he rolled around for breath out there; but if I did it was an entirely dispassionate eye, like the lens of a submarine's periscope. It took him some time to pass me, until he disappeared round the headland to my left, and for some time afterwards I fancied I could hear the regular flop and splashing of his stroke, as one sometimes hears the tread of a ship's engines when it has long sailed out of vision. Since then, whenever I hear such a beat of engines in the night, I think, there goes the French swimmer on his way.

Thrashing as they went

On Ascension Day they beat the bounds of St Michael's Church in Oxford, to establish once again the parish limits and emphasize the old pre-eminence of the Church. Once I followed the course of this antic but moving ceremony. Led by the vicar, a little raggle-taggle group of choirboys and parishioners paraded through the city centre, now and then pausing at immemorially ordained spots to thrash a wall with canes and shout 'Mark! Mark! Mark!' (in the old days they used to thrash the choirboys too, to impress the boundaries on them once and for all). The route they pursued was involved, but the vicar and his crew were not perturbed. Once they scrambled over a high wall, once they marched deadpan through Woolworth's, and once they beat the wall of a banana store in the market. They followed the line to the bitter end, thrashing as they went, as fifteen generations of parsons and giggling choristers had loyally done before them.

Forty tailors and a camel driver

In a little upstairs factory in a Cairo backstreet forty tailors work, year after year, on the vast and splendid carpet, lavishly embroidered with gold thread, that covers the sacred shrine of the Kaaba in Mecca. A new one is woven every year, and is taken to the holy city at the time of the great pilgrimage, escorted by soldiers of the Egyptian army. When I visited the factory the tailors were nearly all Turkish by origin, and nearly all related to one another, and nearly all very old, and some of them represented the third or fourth family generation to work there. They sat at trestle tables in a long rickety room and stitched away there like the tailors of myth. They held their eyes very close to their work, and some of them wore little steel-rimmed spectacles on the ends of their noses. Their director, a portly and paternal official, sauntered up and down the tables with me, and the tailors, working away with their reels of gold thread, threw pleasantries as we passed. I asked one how old he was. As old as the hills, he said, but the director said with pride that he was actually a hundred years old – 'And so,' he added, peering round the room and indicating another benevolent ancient, 'so is the one in the corner, the one with the hat on.' All the old men grinned and nodded.

As we climbed down the staircase to the street, I noticed an elderly Egyptian sitting morosely on a stool outside the door, like a disconsolate watchman, with a white scarf around his head and a string of prayer beads in his lap. Who was he, I wondered. They said that until a few years before the carpet had been taken to Mecca each year on a magnificently caparisoned camel, and the man on the stool had been the camel driver. His unique occupation was gone, and he had never been the same man since. 'Poor fellow,' they said, 'he never leaves the factory' – and when we looked at him, I noticed, he shifted his big feet uneasily.

Singin' in the dawn

Once very early in Beijing I strayed over a bridge to a leafy path beside a moat. I was led there by a curious cacophony of shouts, singing and twanged instruments, and I found it to be a place of self-fulfilment. Resolutely facing a high stone rampart above the moat, like Jews at the Wailing Wall, all along the path men and women were rehearsing their own particular accomplishments privately in the dawn. As we sing in the evening tub, so the people of Beijing go to that wall. Here was a man, his face a few inches from the masonry, declaiming some heroic soliloquy. Here a woman was practising an astonishing range of arpeggios. A splendid bass was singing a romantic ballad, a poet seemed to be trying out a lyric, an elderly man with a bicycle was plucking the strings of an antique lute. I thought of joining in, so universal did these impulses seem, sending To Be or Not to Be reverberating down that wall, or perhaps reciting some of my own purple passages: but I restrained myself, as a Foreign Guest, and just whistled my way home to breakfast.

'I hope you see it truly'

A young forester walked by, as I picnicked by Loch Ness, and I asked him if he had ever seen the monster. He did not smile at the question. He had lived there always, he said, but he had not seen it yet. For him, though, its existence or non-existence was not important, because he interpreted it as a didactic figure of faith. 'It teaches us to believe in something we canna see – you understand me?' He thought a great deal about the matter, he told me, and often looked out there on the half chance of glimpsing the creature. I said I seemed to see it every five minutes, but again he did not laugh. 'Well before you go home,' he said meaningfully, looking me straight in the eye, 'I hope you see it *truly* . . .'

Not altogether intelligible

The holy land of the Yezidis is in the Kurdish country of Iraq, and I was taken to meet some in their village north of Mosul. They follow an unusually cloudy religion concerned with the worship or perhaps propitiation of the devil. They seemed to me distinctly vague about it all, but although they were very hospitable I was haunted throughout my visit by the fear of committing some dreadful spiritual solecism. I must never, I had been told, utter the name Satan, for it is anathema to the devil: if somebody does speak it, the really convinced Yezidi must either instantly kill the transgressor, or commit suicide. Lettuces were strictly taboo: it is said that the Evil One once tried to hide inside a lettuce, but found its leaves insufficient to conceal him. Radishes were also unpopular, I was told, and the colour blue was something the Yezidis particularly loathed. They are most welcoming in everyday affairs, though, and if I wandered up the village stream the house-wives at their washing would smile at me and make jokes (which, being expressed in a corrupt version of medieval Kurdish, were not altogether intelligible to me).

The croupier

I remember clearly the appearance of one of the most famous of the Nevada croupiers. He was a tall man who wore a check shirt, open at the neck, narrow trousers sustained by a belt with an ornate buckle, and a black eyeshade. His face was withered and wrinkled like a tortoise's, his nose hooked and slightly crooked, his eye sharp and pale, his mouth thin but humorous, conveying an impression of very calculated bonhomie. His ears were long and protruding and his long thin neck was entwined with a mesh of muscles, like Laocoön and the snake. Coldly and knowingly this man presided over the game, taking or paying mechanically with never a flicker of emotion, only the slightest hint of a nod, or the suspicion of a gesture, or the embryo trace of a beckon in the direction of the management. In front of him the piles of big silver dollars (common currency in Nevada then) glittered like stage properties; and once in a decade, I dare say, there passed through his hands a dollar made of gold, withdrawn with heart searchings from beneath some aged indigent's mattress.

Mormon faithful

Whenever I think of Salt Lake City, with the pinnacles of the Mormon Temple shining there beneath the mountains, I think of bright clothes and urgent smiles, the voices of the vast Mormon choir ringing across Temple Square on Sunday morning, the unquenchable cheerfulness of the people, the general air of satisfied competence, and the extraordinary blandness of the old lady who told me one fine summer morning that for high religious purposes she had been tracing the course of her ancestry, and had succeeded in establishing it as far back as 64 BC, 'Only a few years,' as she rightly remarked, 'before Caesar went to England, but of course the ancient Americans had been civilized for centuries, as the blessed prophet Moroni told our founder – that's him, that's the prophet Moroni, right up there on the Temple tower – see?' – and I looked up there, shading my eyes against the sun, but could perceive only the vague outline of that antique saint, holding what looked like a trumpet.

His Highness

One fine Arabian morning I walked into the palace of the Sultan of Muscat and Oman, on the shores of the Indian Ocean in Dhufar. Through the great gate of the outer courtyard I passed, and the slaves bowed low, into the polished hall of the palace, lined with bearded and begowned retainers, their rifles in their hands, until there approached me from the darkened recesses of the building a small dignified figure in a brown and gold aba, a turban on his head, a sword at his side, a heavy scent of frankincense emanating from his person. 'Good morning,' said His Highness the Sultan Said bin Taimur.

He was only forty-four, but the voluminous dignity of his robes, his stately bearing and his luxuriant beard all combined to make him look much older. His eyes were large, dark, long-lashed and very serious. His mouth, though kindly and humorous, looked to me capable of an occasional sneer. It was an antique, melancholy face, such you might see in old pictures of the East, and as profoundly enigmatical as the Pyramids. Later I was to encounter him in less autocratic mode, and then his eyes had a soft, thoughtful, almost sleepy look beneath their heavy eyelids, reminding me rather of an elaborately turbaned Cheshire Cat.

Feudalism

If you go down a gold mine, in the South Africa of the 1950s, you will find that racial feudalism extends even to the face of the reef. A black man brings you your boots, helmet and overalls; and a black man hands you your face rag as you enter the hoist; and a black man blows his whistle and drives you in his trolley along the underground corridor; and a black man helps you off with your jacket when, as you approach the stope, the heat of the pit suddenly blasts you. A white Afrikaner overseer grins you a welcome there, but in front of him, flat on his back in an alcove of the rock, is the African driller, helmeted and bathed in sweat at the very war front of the mine. He holds his big drill with his feet, and he lies there like some hefty freak or prodigy, a handless painter or a three-legged man, his whole body shaking with the vibration of the drill, and the very air about him shuddering with its noise. He pauses in his work as you approach, but the supervisor gives him a flicker of his torch, and he is off again, smiling broadly through his dirt.

Merciless fish

At sea in the Caribbean an elderly sailor pointed out to me the dark shadow of a shark, loitering beside the hull of our ship, and this is what he told me: 'It's got no marcy, no marcy at all. Big blue fish, so you can't see 'um in de water, he's sly! No marcy, see, not a drop of marcy!'

Nanny talk

The nannies of the London park were there in their battalions, elderly complacent nannies and perky young ones and hard old professionals with starched faces. 'So I said to her, I said, "No, madam, it is not and never has been my job to make the tea . . ."' 'It's never been the same since Lady Sarah passed over but, there, times have changed, haven't they, dear?' 'No, Jeremy darling, keep away from the doggy, dear . . .' '"Give him his tea?" I said, "I haven't been looking after children for thirty years without knowing when it's teatime," I said, and with that I walked out . . .' 'Try rubbing his back, Mabel, that usually brings it up, doesn't it, dear?'

Chief of the Egyptians

Gamal Abdel Nasser, the President of Egypt, lived blamelessly with his buxom wife and five children in a modest Cairo house that was plain to the point of ugliness. No rude or ranting orator greeted me there, behind some big officious desk. On the contrary, the Chief of the Egyptians was relaxed and friendly, in shirtsleeves, his vest showing between the buttons, and he gave me coffee and talked pleasantly and intelligently for as long as I liked. Nasser like to call himself the first indigenous ruler of Egypt since the Pharaohs, and he was indeed a genuine through-and-through Egyptian, born of peasant stock on the banks of the Nile. 'What a reasonable sort of man,' I said to myself as we talked across the plain deal table, sipping thick chamomile coffee from cups edged with blue roses and gilt.

I was not deceived, though. For many long years Nasser led an underground revolutionary movement, and I knew he had talents of deception and conspiracy of a very high order. His horizons were limitless, and he liked to talk about circles of power, national destinies, the interventions of fate and that sort of thing. The hours slipped smoothly by as he expounded his theories, the coffee cups came and went, until at last the President rose from the table, his sandals flip-flopping across the linoleum, to see me to the door in his shirtsleeves and wave me goodbye into the night. The sentries saluted obsequiously.

Anglo-Sudanese

Good living is a Sudanese tradition, but it came as a disagreeable surprise to me in a Khartoum bar one evening to meet a young Sudanese, just down from the university, drunk not in the Sudanese but in the British manner; facetious with the sweaty banter of his British companions, not with any African drollery, with his tie loosened precisely as theirs was and a cigarette sticking to his lower lip. His grandfather had charged across the plain at Omdurman, brandishing a spear and screaming, but when this modern Sudanese slurred into the maudlin it was the maudlin of smoky pubs and potato crisps. I was shocked. But the British administrators of the Sudan have a wonderful knack of making you feel slightly ashamed of yourself, and I thought of that unlovely young man when I later read in a pamphlet of theirs: 'A new nation is being born, and in the difficult world of today the new arrival needs all the sincere sympathy and disinterested help you can give or get it.'

I blushed: but it did not matter, for all the electric lights had gone out.

An exotic

⌒

Sen Tenzing was a Sherpa who had become well known as a porter with British mountaineering expeditions in the 1930s. He had always been a man of lively tastes, and by the time I met him in Kathmandu, when he was elderly, much respected and semi-retired, his appearance was wonderfully distinctive. On his head he wore a brown balaclava helmet with a peak, like the hats the Red Army used to wear. His grey sports shirt had polished major's crowns upon its epaulettes. Over woollen long johns he wore a voluminous pair of blue shorts, and on his feet were elderly trainers. A confused variety of beads, tokens and Tibetan charms dangled around his neck and a bracelet hung upon his wrist. In one hand he flourished an ice axe, in the other a fly whisk. It was not for nothing that Sen Tenzing, in the old days of gentlemanly climbing, had been affectionately christened

84

by his British employers 'The Foreign Sportsman'.

Mr Beebe

ᴗᴄ

Virginia City, the most famous old mining town of Nevada, has been kept boisterously alive by gambling, and by the presence there of Mr Lucius Beebe. Mr Beebe owns and edits a revived newspaper of the Gold Rush days, the *Territorial Enterprise*, and he lives grandly in a small Victorian mansion, keeping Rolls-Royces and St Bernards. Almost before we had settled in at our hotel he was aware of our presence by bush telegraph, and before long he was showing us the town, wearing a hat with a flat crown and very broad brim, a shirt with a wide and handsome check, an elegant pinstriped suit and a waistcoat embellished with a gold watch-chain. Mr Beebe is a fine sight at any time, but is at his best when he strides into a gambling house with his St Bernard at his heels, pausing for a moment beside a roulette wheel to throw a handful of silver dollars on the table with a satisfying clang, shrugging his shoulders with cheerful nonchalance when he loses the whole lot, bending an ear to a tattered prospector from the hills who has some slight financial worry, raising a negligent hand of greeting to an acquaintance here and there, listening patiently to the report of activities of a man who plans to get even with him for something he published in the paper last week, ushering his guest into the dimness of the bar with a truly Bostonian courtesy before hitching his ample frame on to a bar stool and ordering an enormously large whisky. During our stay in the town Mr Beebe lent us one of his Rolls-Royces, for our convenience.

Battle hardened

کے

'Lucky you got me,' Chicago taxi drivers nearly always seemed to say, if you wanted to visit the tough black neighbourhoods. 'Not many guys would take you. I tell you, I was a Marine for four years, I fought in eight major battles, eight *major* battles, and believe me if any of these blacks get in my way I'll just run 'em down, just like that. Lock your door now. Like I say, it's lucky you found me. Not many guys would come out this way.'

Celebrating with Breughel

کے

If ever you attend a rustic wedding in the Orange Free State you will realize how close the Afrikaner can be to the world of the old Dutch masters. The reception is held in the church hall, and the room is packed, and hot with robust gaiety. At the top table sit the bride and groom, flushed and rotund, she in an ornate white headdress, he intolerably corseted in black. Here are the bride's parents, wrinkled and sharp of face, and here also the two small bridesmaids, their plump country figures wrapped in pink and blue, posed self-consciously beside a potted palm. Big black servants scurry about with cold drinks and sweetmeats. 'It's all done to plan,' says your host complacently. 'All the tables are numbered, you see, so that everyone knows just where to sit – no confusion, you see, no pushing or shoving, everyone can have a good time.' And everyone does. Now and then somebody makes a speech, generally disregarded, and the bride and bridegroom sometimes simper at each other at the demand of amateur photographers, and a hubbub of enjoyment and mastication fills the hall. Each trestle table makes a party of its own and eats its pastries with gusto, and shouts cheerfully for the Africans with the drinks; and the whole scene is warm and homely and animated, with the sheen of red velvet dresses, the fizz of bottled pop, smiling weathered faces, white satin, excited little girls and a smell of flowers and scent and sandwiches.

Shoeshine

The waiter at Colombo put down my breakfast and said he hoped I would have an enjoyable day. I told him I was going to make a pilgrimage to the grave of my father-in-law, a planter who had died in Ceylon during the war.

'By God,' he said at once, 'that's good, that's very good – parents is a bigger thing than the Lord Buddha himself,' and picking up my shoes, to clean them for the occasion, he bowed gracefully and withdrew.

We did not linger

With an American colleague I once went to a ceremony at Alexandria at which some new Czech weapons were to be handed over to the Egyptian forces. In those days many German specialists and advisers were working for the Egyptian army, and as we waited for the ceremony to begin we noticed a crowd of Egyptian officers milling around a tall figure in a black beret at the corner of the grandstand. We elbowed our way across and found ourselves face to face with as obvious and disagreeable a Nazi officer as ever I saw. His face was congealed with hauteur; his movements were stiff and mechanical, like a robot's; and icy cold were the eyes with which, flicking his cane against his long legs, he turned to look at us. The jostling Egyptians crowded admiringly all around him, but my colleague was a Jew, and we did not linger.

A family outing

It was a festival day of some kind, and in the evening I asked a taxi driver in Beirut to take me for a run around the neighbouring hills, to observe the village goings-on. He brought along his family for the ride – a plump smiling wife in black, a little boy in jeans and a very small baby girl with enormous brown eyes. The driver had spent some years in America, and his English was sprinkled with rather dated Americanisms – 'Say, what you say we stop for a sundae?' or 'How d'ya feel like a Coke, baby?' – as we progressed through the balmy evening. We frequently stopped in villages for some quick refreshment among the celebrations. Candles were burning in many windows, and there was a constant crackling of fireworks and whizzing of rockets. Gangs of young men strolled about the hilly streets, singing and shouting. Innumerable friends and relatives of the taxi driver emerged from houses to impede our progress, and we had so many bottles of pop that the baby was visited by a staccato series of burps. 'What feast day is this?' I asked the driver. 'Christmas, friend,' he replied (it was the middle of July).

When we started our journey back the family was fast asleep in the back seat, in a tangle of ungainly abandon, and the driver and I smiled at each other. 'Dig those crazy guys,' said he, as another festive party rollicked by.

Tactful parent

During my stay in Darjeeling I often saw a young American dressed in the habit of a Buddhist monk. He was studying at a nearby seminary, I was told, and wore the brown cloak, the sandals and the hair bun as to the manner born. Nobody appeared in the least surprised by this anomalous figure, and his father, who was paying him a visit from the States, seemed entirely at home with the turn of family events. 'I'm going to drink, Jimmy,' I heard him saying to his son one day, puffing at his cigar and raising his glass, 'I'm going to drink to all these wonderful, wonderful people of Darjeeling!' (And 'Say,' he tactfully added as he put his glass down, rather hastily I thought, 'is this Indian wine? *Delicious!*')

A small magnifico

I was strolling through the souk in Qatar when there emerged from a doorway beside me the smallest man I had ever seen. He was about four feet high, stout and prosperous looking, dressed in the resplendent regalia of an Arab gentle-man – splendid brown aba, milk-white keffiyeh, black head-band, dagger and beads. With a flourish and a toss of his head this marvellous figure strode down the steps of his house and swaggered away through the souk, as bold and assured as any gigantic African chieftain or Renaissance aristocrat. His proud head bobbed away among the packing cases, and a breath of the incense that perfumed his beard hung in the bazaar behind him.

A large magnifico

'Back again,' said the magnifico at the cafe on the last ridge before Cetinje and the heart of Montenegro. We had met before, you see. He is always there, it seems, summer or winter, like a major-domo of these uplands, or a Chief of Protocol. He wears black breeches, and a wide belt like a cummerbund, and he stands about seven feet tall, and speaks in a basso profundo, and tosses slivovic back like lime juice, and is in all respects the very model of a modern Montenegran.

A snatch of sound in Morocco

'Go to sleep now,' they said, 'the operation will be later.'
But when they had gone I got out of bed rather shakily,
for the drug was beginning to work,
and went to say goodbye to myself in the mirror.
As I did so a street vendor outside played a delicate
arpeggio upon his flute,
a very gentle merry sound
which he repeated, over and over again,
in sweet diminuendo down the street.
Flights of angels, I said to myself, and so
staggered to my bed, and oblivion.

'Ain't that right?'

⌒

In Montana once I found the road blocked for a mile or more by a mass of sheep. Some were moving very slowly, some were nibbling the sparse grass beside the highway, some were sitting down and one or two seemed to be fast asleep. At the head of this leisurely procession were two cowboys, mounted on fine black horses. The men were very weatherbeaten, dirty and bearded, with their tangled hair escaping from their hats and their fingernails black and broken. They had been rounding up the sheep in the surrounding mountains, to bring them down for shearing and to escape the coming winter storms. 'We been fourteen days in the hills,' said one, 'and seven days on the move. Sheep ain't very fast movers. Boy, will I be glad of a bed!

'As for this horse,' he added affectionately, 'all he wants is a good hot cup of coffee and a place to put his feet up. Ain't that right, boy?'

In a trance?

When I was alone in the Himalaya one day I saw a man. I saw him first in the extreme distance, across an absolutely blank snowfield at about 19,000 feet, to which I had climbed from the glacier below for the sake of the view. At first I could not make out what he was – only a black swaying speck, indescribably alone in the desolation. As he came closer I could see that he could only be human, so I plunged through the loose snow to meet him, and presently, there near the top of the world, thousands of feet and many miles above the trees, we met face to face. It was the strangest encounter of my life.

He was a holy man, wandering in the mountains, I suppose, for wandering's sake. His brown, crinkled, squashed-up face looked back at me expressionless from beneath a yellow hood, and seemed to find nothing strange in my presence there. He wore a long yellow cloak and hide boots, and from his waist there hung a spoon and a cloth satchel. He carried nothing else, and he wore no gloves. I greeted him as best I could, but he did not answer, only smiling at me distantly and without surprise. Perhaps he was in a trance.

I offered him a piece of chocolate but he did not take it, simply standing there before me, slightly smiling. Presently we parted, and without a word he continued on his unfaltering journey, making, it seemed, for Tibet without visible means of survival and moving with a proud, gliding and effortless motion that seemed inexorable. He did not appear to move fast, but when I looked round he had almost disappeared, and was no more than that small black speck again, inexplicably moving over the snows.

The truth of it

In a churchyard in County Monaghan I stood beside the grave of Seamus McElwain, a young IRA man whose whole life had been a succession of bloodshed and imprisonments until he had been killed by British soldiers in a neighbouring meadow. His epitaph was in Irish, and on the cross, together with the relief of a bird escaping through a mesh of barbed wire, was affixed a coloured photograph of him, a good-looking dark-haired boy in a dinner jacket. The tears came into my eye as I stood there (the wind rustling the hedges all around), and a gardener working nearby asked me if perhaps I was a McElwain myself? But I said I was simply crying for them all, whatever side they were on. 'That's the truth of it,' he said, 'that's the truth.'

Urgent inquiries

Wide eyed and open handed the Fijians greet me, in their tidy thatched settlements off the highway, or among the mangrove swamps where the women, hitching their skirts up to their waists, scoop about indelicately for shellfish. 'Where are you going? What is your name? Are you married? Where do you live? Have you any children? Would you like a banana? How many people live in London? Do you sleep alone?' Their inquiries are directed urgently at me: the Fijian for curiosity is *via kila* – knowledge want. I told the maids in my Suva hotel that I was scared of them, because they stared at me so hard, and in the evening I found a little bowl of flowers placed beneath my window in appeasement. 'Aaah,' they said, shaking their big kind heads in remorse, 'we no wish to frighten you.'

Their forebears used to be cannibals, but I would not mind being eaten in Fiji. The pot would be spiced, the cooking gentle, and the occasion in most ways merry.

On the waterfront

After a day around the docks with the notorious Manhattan longshoremen, still among the more obstreperous of the city's workers, I thought of them with more sympathy. That evening I took a coffee and doughnut in a diner down there, and tried to imagine what it would have been like to be a poor Irish immigrant half a century ago, looking for work on that hard and dirty shore. When the man on the next stool scowled across the napkin stand and said nastily, 'You want all the sugar?' I told myself he was the victim of historical circumstance, and said I was most awfully sorry.

Empire builders?

I loved to sit on a Hong Kong ferry and contemplate the remaining Britons of Hong Kong. They were trapped for me there, like historical specimens, deep in their tabloids or compiling their shopping lists. What a line they represented, I used to think! What generations of exile culminated in their persons, listlessly looking out across the passing harbour, or doing the crossword puzzle! Their forefathers blazed a way across the world, veld to outback, pioneering in shacks, beachcombing on reefs, disciplining recalcitrant Sioux or bayoneting fuzzy-wuzzies; and there they were beside me, the last of the long parade, indifferent to their origins, unconscious of them, perhaps, unexcited on the slat-seated ferryboat between Kowloon and Victoria!

The boat shudders; the gangplanks clatter down; the blue-shirted Chinese seamen swing open the iron gates; and in a trice, as the crowd streams off the vessel, those unobtrusive imperialists are so utterly overwhelmed by their Chinese fellow citizens that you would hardly guess there was a Briton left in Hong Kong at all.

Icelandic allegory

Beauty and the Beast is an Icelandic allegory. Everybody who goes to the island is struck by the splendour of the girls. Pick a choice example now – the shop girl, say, who is packing your stuffed puffin in the souvenir shop, or pricing your lava-stone powder box. What a gorgeous strapping girl she is, what a terrific golden girl, with her wide-apart eyes, her hair bleached in Arctic sunshine, her exquisite complexion mixed out of snow and pink blossom!

Take your eyes off her for a moment, though, and observe the young man shambling down the street outside – towards his trawler, perhaps, or off to his fearful shift at the fish factory. He is the original Viking, I suppose. His forehead and his chin symmetrically recede, his cheeks are wolfishly sunken, his eyes blaze, and there is to his loping walk a suggestion of immense loose-limbed power, as though a tap on his shoulder would unleash his double-bladed battleaxe and send him off to Greenland with horns on his head.

Wedding pictures

When King Hussein of Jordan married it was supposed to be a ceremony of liberated modernity. However, as I joined the society ladies for the occasion I could not help feeling that we were close in spirit to the huddled jealousies and school-girl excitements of the harem. At the head of the stairs were two bold lancers in scarlet tunics and white breeches, as the eunuchs would have stood sentry in an earlier age, and the body of the room was a seething mass of women. They were dressed magnificently, a glitter of satins and brocades and furs, a mosaic of lipsticks and mascaras, a tinkling kaleido-scope of earrings, a flurry of sequinned handbags. Chanel and Dior thickened the air. How often and how brazenly did the women of the court eye each other's coutures! How heavily accentuated were the outlines of their eyes, like eyes seen through diaphanous curtains in forbidden corridors of the Seraglio! How scratchy and talon-like were the finger-nails, how pinkly fleshy the figures, and how passive and doll-like those emancipated ladies looked, in serried and perfumed phalanx, as if some lascivious Sultan were about to pass through their ranks, picking a beauty here and a beauty there with a lordly gesture of his forefinger!

But presently a cameraman in a crumpled jacket sudden-ly pressed his way past the guards and said (as it were), 'Just one more, ladies, please, give us a nice smile now.'

A holy clock

In the Church of the Holy Sepulchre at Jerusalem a little chapel stands shrouded in black curtains beside the site of the sepulchre itself. One morning I found myself all alone before this shrine, and as I stood there in the silence I thought I heard a faint ticking noise from the inside. For a moment I stood hesitant, thinking it might be the working of a perpetual censer, or perhaps the swinging of an ornate lantern on its chain. But it was so regular and so insistent that I pulled the heavy curtains aside and looked in, and there on the altar, all alone among the ikons and candlesticks, a red moon-faced kitchen clock ticked away robustly, for all the world as though it were timing the eggs. I laughed with pleasure at this unexpected discovery, and there was an answering chuckle behind my back. Standing among the tall pillars of the rotunda, all but hidden in the shadows, there stood a gigantic Abyssinian priest in an attitude of serene meditation. When I turned to look at him a white gleam in the darkness testified to the smile upon his black bearded face.

Silly question

Wildness, freeness, recklessness – not in Vienna! I went to a police court there one day and, noticing one of the accused studying a road map between hearings, asked him if he was planning an escape. 'No,' he said, 'I am deciding the best route to visit my aunt at Graz.'

Expertise

⌒

I visited the Pioneer Museum, in Fremont County, Wyoming. During my visit a schoolmistress was taking a group of children round the exhibits, and I heard her drawing their attention to a chair that stood in a corner of the gallery. It was made all of bleached white horn: legs, seat, back and all. 'That is an example', she was saying, 'of the craftsmanship of the very first pioneers to come to Fremont County. Isn't that beautiful, children?' 'Yes, ma'am,' most of them replied, but after the main body had moved on to the Shoshone relics, a section of the museum I preferred to circumvent, I noticed a pair of laggard urchins trailing along behind. They had not heard their teacher's encomium of the chair, but they too paused as they passed it, and inspected it with no less knowledgeable admiration. 'Jeez,' said one to the other. 'Take a look at that elk.'

First time lucky!

⌒

I crossed to Hoboken on the very last voyage of the very last Manhattan railroad ferry, and the shabby old boat was full for the occasion with reporters, cameramen, roistering office workers, people with banners and leaflets and comic hats and crates of champagne, and a trio of Salvation Army girls singing unaccompanied hymns indefatigably above the hubbub. I sat down on a grubby bench beside an elderly habitué of the ferry. 'You sound kinda British,' he said. 'Funny place for you to be, ain't it? You ride this boat regular?'

'Never before in my life,' said I.

'Well, you don't say. Some people have it easy. I've had to ride this ferry forty years to make the last crossing. You come over and do it first time!'

Advice

By and large, it seemed to me, British businessmen in Hong Kong pursued their various careers in a pleasant state of half-speed ahead, eating well, enjoying their friends, gossiping in the club bar, taking the junk out on Sundays – 'Whatever you do,' they used to tell me, 'don't go out with Bill [or Simon, or Ted], you'll be drunk before you get out of the harbour.'

Racial tension

Six or seven miles out of Pretoria, on my way to catch an early flight, I saw a black figure running helter-skelter down the road towards the city. A moment later another followed, and then two or three more, and they panted by us, with serious faces and bulging eyes, like participants in some strenuous sunrise celebration.

'What are they doing?' I asked my driver.

'Those Kaffirs? They're on their way to work. They've probably got to start at seven, and they've got a long way to go, so they've got to run fast. It won't do them any harm.'

'You don't like Kaffirs?' I surmised.

'Kaffirs?' he replied with a genial twinkle. 'I love them like they was vermin.'

Kurds on the move

How's this for a glimpse? Once, once only, I encountered a tribe of Kurds on the move. It was spring, the grasslands were thick with flowers, and in the distance the mountain barriers stood blue and purple and formidable, with a fleck of snow on their summits and a cloudless sky above. Against this heavenly background the Kurdish nomads moved triumphantly across my field of vision. Their herds of sheep and floppy-eared goats scrambled and jostled in the sunshine, and behind them the bold horsemen lorded it across the plain, riding their stocky horses like avenging marauders, rifles across their backs, bandoliers across their chests, sheepskin jackets slung about them grandly. The women walked alongside, carrying the baggage; the children scampered or lagged behind; the great herds eddied about and spilled over the landscape; and the effect of the procession, glimpsed in so wide and airy a setting, was that of a community of unusually cheerful brigands crossing a steppe to commit an atrocity.

Before fame hit him

A couple of days after Edmund Hillary and Tenzing Norkay became the first climbers ever to reach the summit of Everest, I was near the foot of the mountain on my way home. It was a still, oppressive, grey morning, and I saw away up the glacier, coming down from the mountain, a solitary figure moving swiftly and gracefully down the valley, swinging and buoyant, like some unspoilt mountain creature. A wide-brimmed hat! High reindeer boots! A smile that illuminated the glacier! An outstretched hand of greeting! Tenzing!

He took off his big hat, smiling still, and sat down upon a rock. He was going to rest and wash, he said, and then traverse a neighbouring ridge towards his home village, where his mother lived. We had breakfast together, and he pulled from his wallet a snapshot of himself with a number of little Tibetan terriers. 'Given me by the Dalai Lama,' he explained with pride, and taking a pen from his pocket he slowly wrote his signature (the only word he could write) across the bottom of it and handed it to me with a deprecatory grin. The last I saw of him there, he had stripped his lean lithe body to the waist and was soaping himself with water from a tin basin. It looked a chilly operation.

By the very next day he would be one of the most famous men on earth.

'Mamma mia!'

A veteran fisherman took me out into the Venetian lagoon to find an island house I had read about, but when we reached the spot we found that nothing remained of it but a pile of rubble. The old man was astonished, but even more affronted. 'Now why should a thing like that happen?' he asked me indignantly. '*Mamma mia!* That house was there when I was a child, a fine big house of stone – and now it's gone! Now why should that have happened, eh? Tell me that!'

He was an urbane man, though, beneath his stubble, and as we moved away from that desolate place, and turned our prow towards San Pietro, I heard a rasping chuckle from the stern of the boat. '*Mamma mia!*' the old man said again, shaking his head from side to side: and so we chugged home laughing and drinking wine until, paying insufficient attention to his task, that fisherman ran us aground and broke our forward gear, and we completed the voyage pottering shamefacedly backwards. 'Like a couple of crabs,' he said, unabashed, 'though even the crabs go sideways.'

An apartheid queue

In the evening all the poor black workers of Johannesburg, forbidden to live within the precincts of the city, rush for the buses that will take them to their slums and sprawling estates. You can hardly watch such a scene without the stirring of some crusading instinct, some Byronic impulse, or at least a stab of pity. As dusk falls, and as the bitter winter night begins to whistle through the buildings, a vast tattered queue moves in raggety parade towards the bus depot, and thousands of Africans shuffle their slow way in double file towards their shabby buses. There is an air of unutterable degradation to the scene, so heartless and machine-like is the progress of the queue, as the white folk hasten off in their cars to the rich city districts, and the lights glitter in the windows of the department stores, and those poor lost souls are crammed into their buses and packed off to their distant ill-lit townships. Many of them are half starving. Most of them live in fear of robbery or violence when they step off the buses into the dark streets of the locations; half of them spend almost all their leisure hours travelling between the city and the far-flung patches of high veld in which they are obliged to live; they reach their homes long after dark at night, and they start work again when the morning is still only a suggestion.

Old-school flying

In earlier days of transatlantic flying it was generally necessary for passenger aircraft to refuel en route, at Gander in Newfoundland, Shannon in Ireland, or somewhere or other on the way to San Francisco. I was travelling to America on a British Overseas Airways Corporation aircraft when we were told that because of favourable winds we would not for once have to make an intermediate stop. About halfway across, the aircraft's captain came chattily around the passenger cabins, as was the BOAC custom, in the full glory of his regalia – they ran their planes like ships then, and he was very much the Master.

'Everything all right?' he asked courteously, in a clipped public-school accent, when he came to me. 'Having a comfortable flight?'

'Everything's fine,' I told him, 'but there is one thing: are you quite sure you've got enough fuel to get us over without a stop?'

'Never fear,' he replied in the best old-school British style. 'We're terrible cowards up front.'

Festivities!

On Princes Street that day, when the Edinburgh Festival was

in full fling, half a dozen sideshows were performing. An old-fashioned socialist demagogue was haranguing the crowd from his soapbox. A man in full evening dress was singing 'On the Sunny Side of the Street' from the steps of the National Gallery. Two comedians dressed as ancient Egyptians were doing a comic act, and a tipsy old fellow in a kilt was dancing a reel to the music of a wind-up gramophone. All of a sudden amidst the hubbub two young toughs in shirtsleeves struck up a bit of a fight, punching each other in a tentative way and exchanging high-pitched Scottish insults. Instantly all attention turned to them. The orator found his audience dwindling before his eyes, the ancient Egyptians were soon playing to an empty pavement, and swirling here and there across the pavement went all the audiences, wavering and staggering with each exchange of blows. Through the melee, as it disappeared behind the Scott Memorial, I could see the fierce squabbling heads of the contestants, mouthing festive curses.

Aloofly towards the dawn

I once heard a pair of Venetian inebriates passing my window at four o'clock on a May morning, and looking out into the Rio San Trovaso I saw them riding by in a gondola. They were sitting on the floor of the boat, drumming on its floorboards, banging its seats, singing and shouting incoherently at the tops of their thickened voices; but on the poop of the gondola, rowing with an easy, dry, worldly stroke, an elderly grey-haired gondolier propelled them aloofly towards the dawn.

Mother Russia

_◟◞_

In Soviet Russia during the Cold War the foreign writer was generally at the mercy of Intourist, the government tourist organization. It was efficient and courteous enough, though speckled no doubt with agents of counter-intelligence, and its younger employees were often refreshingly undogmatic. Now and then, though, Intourist would send you an interpreter of the old school, a woman of severe bearing and inflexible party loyalty. Polite but unmistakably chill such a lady was likely to be, as though you were an emissary of capitalist encirclement, and a day with such an ideologue could be exhausting. I found there was a solution, though, an exorcism. When my companion was particularly severe about my bourgeois deviations, I would turn to her with an expression of deeply wounded sensibility, allow the warm tears to well into my eyes, sniff a little, blow my nose shakily, and tell her I thought she had been _unkind_.

This was a magic word. Instantly there would be released from her bosom a flood of immemorial Russian emotion, dimly lit with ikons and scented with incense. In a trice all thought of norms and Seven-Year Plans would be driven from her kindly mind, and she was likely to be on the telephone half the night, making sure I was warm enough.

'Nobody's used this cup'

_◟◞_

One of the notorieties of the Cape of Good Hope is the 'tot' system, which legally allows a wine farmer to pay his coloured labourers partly in cheap sweet wine. 'You're just in time,' a Huguenot farmer told me when I asked to watch the process. 'We give them six tots a day, you see – one when they start, one at breakfast, one at eleven, one at two, one at four and one when they finish work.'

There stood the labourers in a quavering crew, seven or eight tattered coloured men, and on the steps of a barn a white overseer was doling out the tots. He had a big bucket of thick red wine before him, and as the workers came shambling up with their old baked-bean tins he scooped them their ration in silence. It was an eerie spectacle, for it was plain to me that those dazed and ragged half-castes were in a state of perpetual dissipation. Quaffing their tots in one experienced and joyless gulp they shuffled away again. It was as though eight elderly machines were being greased or refuelled.

'Yes, we give them six tots a day,' said the farmer chattily, 'that's the law. It comes to a bottle and a quarter a day. They sweat it out very quickly – it gives them kick, you see. It's a good wine – here, taste it.' And with fastidious courtesy the foreman, producing a tin cup from inside the barn, wiped it carefully with his handkerchief and drew me a ration. 'It's quite all right,' he said kindly, 'nobody's used this cup.'

Expatriatism

Almost anywhere in the world of the 1950s I met expatriate Britons of the upper bourgeoisie, and almost always they liked to tell me their memories, personal or inherited, factual or fictionalized, of an England long extinct: a garden party England it seemed to have been, where nobody talked too loud, and there were parasols on the lawn, and we so often used to visit Sir Henry . . . Sir Henry . . . what was his name now? – Never mind, I shall remember it later – Anyway, he had this lovely old house. Oh, the smell of the honeysuckle and such gay tennis parties we used to have. 'Of course I know it's all changed now and I could never go back, it would break my heart to see it all so different, socialism, and strikes, and white girls with black men in the streets, they tell me, and all these death duties and so on. But it will always be home to me, Mr Morris – you may be a *little* too young to understand just how I feel – that's Lindley Hall there, by the way, above the mantelpiece, painted by Robert . . . Robert . . . you know, very famous – but I'll remember later, I always do . . .'

On second thoughts

When I was writing a book about Oxford I read that a special duty of the High Steward of Oxford University was 'to hear and determine criminal cases of the gravest kind, like treason or felony', if the accused was a resident member of the university. In legal theory it meant that until capital punishment was finally abolished in England, this purely academic official was authorized to hang you.

I once told a proctor, one of the intendants of university discipline, that I proposed to follow him and his officers (popularly called Bulldogs) on their patrol through the streets one night, to see how the undergraduates responded to his authority. He advised me not to follow too closely, in case the Bulldogs took offence at my attentions, and summoned me into the proctorial presence. I bristled a bit at this. They'd better not, I said, I was a free citizen, I knew my rights, I could walk where I liked when I liked, nobody could pull antique usage over my eyes, he and his minions certainly had no authority over me. The proctor smiled darkly. 'Are you quite sure?' he inquired; and by heavens, remembering the bit about the High Steward and the felonies, on second thoughts I wasn't.

Alas, proved right

I was never a very astute political observer, and I really did not know what to make of Jack Kennedy, the 35th President of the United States, when I went to one of his Washington press conferences soon after his inauguration. I was charmed by the look, sound and presence of him, as everyone was. I was impressed by his professionalism and his fluency, but some vague instinct told me that although he was only in his mid-forties he was already in his prime. In a report I wrote for the *Guardian* I tried to express my feeling that the Kennedy we were seeing then was the definitive Kennedy, that we would never know him greatly changed by time or experience, and, as it sadly happened, for once I was proved right.

A Mikado

Sir Charles Dalrymple Belgrave was officially Adviser to the Ruler of Bahrain, but in effect he was prime minister as well, while Lady Belgrave enjoyed the beguiling title of Directoress of Female Education. For thirty years Belgrave had guided the destinies of the island, and his influence was all pervasive. A mere mention of the name Belgrave would instantly bring a price down. There was a street called Belgrave Road, and not a soul in the place, not a sheikh or a tailor or a man picking his teeth on the high curved prow of a dhow, who could not direct you to the house where the Belgraves lived.

This Mikado viewed his own eminence with a trace of dry amusement, and his home (above his office) was a gay and racy place. Belgrave had a splendid and eclectic library, and he was a man of esoteric tastes, addicted to (for example) roulette, cigars, watercolour painting, swords and pantomimes. Each year he presented a panto of his own in the dining room, with bold backcloths painted by himself and dialogue verging upon the risqué. It was curious that his effect upon his bailiwick was almost sanctimonious. 'How good are roads are,' the island seemed to say, 'and how sensible our schools are, and how thriftily we use our oil royalties. Mohammed, stop picking your nose in front of Lady Belgrave.'

Beggars and buskers

The indigenous beggars and buskers of Venice are treated with indulgence. There is a dear old lady, bundled in shawls, who sits in the evening at the foot of the Accademia bridge, and has many faithful patrons. There is a bent old man who haunts the alleys near Santo Stefano and who is often to be seen pacing from one stand to another, plucking a neat little melody upon his guitar. On Sunday mornings a faun-like couple of countrymen materialize on the quayside of

Giudecca with a set of bagpipes and a wooden whistle. A well-known comic figure of the Zattere is a man in a cloth cap and a long blue overcoat who suddenly appears among the tables of the outdoor cafes and, planting himself in an uncompromising posture on the pavement, legs apart, head thrown back, produces a sheet of music from his pocket and throws himself into a loud incomprehensible aria, tuneless and spasmodic, but delivered with such an air of informed authority that there are often a few innocents to be seen following the melodic line with knowledgeable attention. I once asked this man if I could see his music, and discovered it to be a specimen page from a score of Beethoven's 9th, held upside-down and close to the stomach.

Among the Delhi Spearmen

Among the officers of the 9th Queen's Royal Lancers there was a powerful sense of family. It was hardly like being in an army at all. Age was disregarded and rank was tacit. Nobody called anybody 'sir'. The Colonel was Colonel Jack, or Colonel Tony. Everyone else was known by his Christian name. Courtesy towards each other was not a deliberate form, it was merely a matter of habit, or convenience. This was a very professional regiment. A sense of heritage accordingly bound us one to another, and made us conscious of lance and plume, saddle-carbine and cuirass. These were the Delhi Spearmen; and though the details of the regimental history were less than vivid to most of us, still there hung always around our mess a general suggestion of glory (not that anyone would have been so insensitive as to mention it, for if there was one attribute the 9th Lancers were not anxious to display, it was *keenness*).

Mixed sensations

It seems only the other day that communism ended in Romania, but here I am already at the dinner table with a jolly crew of acquaintances, eating pike-perch from the Danube and drinking a happy Moldavian Riesling, to the deafeningly amplified thump of a band in the chandeliered dining room of the Central House of the Army. I have poked my nose into several such unpromising bastions of old Establishment. At the Writers' Union, for instance, which has been for several decades a tribunal of communist orthodoxy, I wandered bemused and unhindered through the accumulated cigar smoke of a thousand ideological debates, amiably nodded at now and then by marvellously literary-looking confrères. And at the Military Hotel, strolling in, I was befriended without question by a most formidable captain of the Romanian navy, wearing over his gilded uniform a leather coat like a U-boat commander. It is a queer mixture of sensations. On the one hand nearly everybody is welcoming. On the other hand few seem altogether frank.

Sharing the pleasure

In Wyoming cowboys sometimes walked their horses up to me as I picnicked in the sage, sat sketching in my car or took my morning walk through the scented countryside; and then, after we had exchanged pleasantries and told each other where we came from, and explained what we were doing, sometimes they would slide from their saddles and join me for a few minutes, looking over my shoulder at a sketch, accepting a slice of cheese, or simply sharing the pleasure of the place and the moment – not a talkative presence usually, but one so naturally kind and unembarrassed that a silence was never awkward, and the parting came organically, like the end of a good meal, just before satisfaction moved towards surfeit.

Siren call

Seen from Hong Kong's New Territories in those days, China seemed to me essentially *simple*, like a world stripped of its complexities and pretensions. I found myself looking towards that silent landscape as though it were calling me home. Home to where? Home to what? As I wandered down the track towards my car, one of the stall sellers spoke to me quietly, without urgency, across his wares. 'Why don't you buy,' he inquired, as though he genuinely, if mildly, wanted to know the answer, 'the thoughts of Chairman Mao?' – and he held up a small red book, bound in plastic.

'Get thee behind me,' I said.

Valleys music

I prefer to catch a Welsh male voice choir at practice, when it has not been stiffened up with clean shirts and clasped hands for a concert. Nobody ever tried harder than a choir of the valleys intent on getting an interpretation absolutely right. Just once more, cries the conductor – *Unwaith eto, bois!* – and the lady accompanist stiffens herself again at the piano, the stocky tenors, the well-paunched basses adjust their spectacles, smooth out the creases in their music sheets and wait in tense taut postures, like tennis players awaiting a service, for the drop of the baton. The rustlings and the coughings stop. Silence falls. The maestro crouches there before his men, half doubled on the dais, a demoniac figure, black of hair, swarthy of face, eyes gleaming. He is irresistible! He raises his baton. The choir takes a breath. The pianist lifts her fingers. Crash, the place reverberates, the whole town surely, perhaps the whole of Wales, with the passion of the opening chord.

R.I.P.

The foreign news editor, my immediate superior at *The Times*, was ageing, and week by week I noticed not merely a faltering in the old gentleman himself, but a progressive disregard of his views. People did not listen to him. Decisions were taken without his knowledge. He clearly sensed it too, and for what seems to have been hours at a time, talking in an infinitely slow grating voice that was, I admit, among the heavier of my burdens, he would disclose to me his anxieties or more often his resentments.

He grew increasingly talkative, bitter and confused, until finally, one winter evening, he gave me a letter. If anything should happen to him, he said, buttoning his thick black overcoat, straightening his homburg and removing his walking stick from its stand behind the desk, I was to hand it to the higher authorities of *The Times*; and gently chewing – for he generally seemed to have in his mouth, when not a cigar, some kind of lubricant lozenge, perhaps to keep his voice going – he nodded at me in his usual way, said goodnight with his habitual icy trace of a smile, and went home to kill himself with sleeping pills.

Levantine life

I was happy working for the Arab News Agency in Cairo. My friends were mostly in the office, and we were none of us rich. We were boulevardiers, but of a modest rank, frequenting the shabbier of the downtown pavement cafes, murky places with marble-topped tables where the coffee was as thick as porridge and the water glasses were a perpetual dingy grey. There we would sit and talk in the early evening, when the long siesta was nearly over, until we heard the rattle of the heavy steel shutters being raised one by one from the shop fronts, and it was time for us to saunter to the office and start work on the evening bulletin.

The news that greeted us up there was always full of drama and piquant intelligence – wars and corruptions, desert crime, court conspiracies, religious polemics, family feuds – and we worked in a spirit of Bohemian release. Once we were inside our dim-lit, crowded and untidy rooms we would forget the truth about ourselves, forget the impending misery of the midnight tram, forget the shabby villa off the airport road, forget the swarming children and the skinny black-veiled wife, forget our lost hopes for a career in the law or the Ministry of the Interior, forget that we were indigent Egyptian effendis or struggling Levantines, forget even our sexual ambiguities, and lose ourselves in that strange little world of ours upstairs.

America verbatim

From my notebooks:
'I told him, I said, "Johnnie, if you want me you've just gotta come right down here and get me . . ."'
'Crooked? Crooked as a green snake . . .'
'She said that? She actually said that, right there? She said that to your face . . .?'
'Listen, Ed, I'll blind you, honest I will, I'll cut your tongue you old son of a gun you . . .'
'She says to me, "Leon," she says, "I wantya to know, I'm fond of you, truly I am, but there's this problem of Juan's baby, see?" "To hell with Juan's baby," I says. "What's Juan's baby to me?" And she says, "Leon, honey," she says, "listen to me . . ."'
'If Consolidated Edison could be boiled down into one man I wouldn't have him in my home . . .'

An indistinct saint

St Frideswide was an indistinct medieval divine who is the titular saint of Oxford Cathedral. Every 19 October the bigwigs of the city and the diocese process, begowned, befurred, cassocked, epauletted and even bewigged, to celebrate her memory at her shrine in the building. When I was once at the service I noticed that one of the most venerable canons of the cathedral showed signs of irritable impatience. He scowled, muttered audibly to himself, hitched his hood, twitched his surplice, nudged his companions and occasionally gazed frowardly around the congregation. It was true that 'Jerusalem, My Happy Home' did seem more than usually protracted that day, with so much civic weight to slow it down. I watched that clergyman closely, though, and after a time I reached the conclusion that he was not annoyed by the music, only by the occasion. He didn't dislike the hymn tune. He had doubts about the saint.

Mayor Murphy's inducements

It happened that while I was in town St John's, Newfoundland, was celebrating its centenary as a municipality. The festivities closed with a public party which suggested to me an enormous country wedding – everyone someone else's sister-in-law, everyone ready to talk, with no pretence and no pretension either. Jigs and folk songs sounded from the stage, and when people seemed slow to dance jolly Mayor Murphy took the floor alone, offering free booze coupons to any who would join him. 'You have to get them half tight,' he remarked to me as he handed out these inducements, jigging the while himself.

Later I was walking along a city street when a man launched upon me, without warning, a challenging statement in such advanced Newfoundlandese that I can only reproduce it impressionistically, so to speak. It sounded something like: 'Sish yarkin trapse John Murphy.' He looked at me expectantly for a response, so I simultaneously shook my head and nodded, to be on the safe side.

Things to attend to

The millionaire, a man of taste as well as power, commanding everything that money can buy – even he seemed restless and impatient; not socially, for he was kindness itself, but temperamentally. The whole luxurious establishment seemed to me somehow disposable: the manservant, the housekeeper, the masterpieces on the walls, the carpets from the East, the gorgeous maps and the calf-bound library, the great silver tray of decanters and silver-topped siphons, the bronze picked up from an unknown but infinitely promising young sculptor in West Africa – none of it seemed destined to last. It was as though he might decide one day to rip it all up and start again. As he saw me off at the door two things happened. An alarm buzzer sounded, announcing that the eldest son of the house had got stuck in the elevator, and the millionaire's wife called through the drawing-room door to say that the White House was on the telephone. 'Excuse me,' he said in his flat velvet voice, shaking hands on the doorstep. 'I have one or two things to attend to. Thanks for coming.'

Give and take

One still hears the instant give and take in Dublin pubs and parlours. 'Ah, me rheumatism's cured,' says the old lady quick as a flash when the landlord pats her kindly on the knee, 'you should advertise your healing powers.' 'Sure it was only my left hand too,' says the landlord. 'Well and it was only my left knee – try the other one there's a good man.'

The judge

The judge at the Court of Session, Scotland's High Court, wore his tight-curled wig as though it had sprouted spontaneously from his pate in childhood. Crouched over his papers at his high dais, he was big nosed, wrinkle eyed, high cheeked, hooded, with eyes that never seemed to blink, and a mouth that expressed, whatever interrogation he supervised, whatever sentence he was decreeing, no flicker of concern, distaste or even particular interest. I could seldom hear what he said, for he spoke in a cracked and high-pitched drone apparently outside my aural range, but I observed that, like an owl peering down from a telephone wire, he missed no nuance or allusion of the proceedings below him. When I left the court I turned at the door for one last fascinated look at him, and discovered that, although his slumped posture had apparently not budged an inch, those pale blue eyes of his were staring fixed and motionless into mine – rather as though, like the owl, he could rotate his head without reference to his body, preparatory to dismembering a mouse.

Across a chasm

~~

All the windows in the huge slab of a building are brilliantly lit, and in each a little cameo, separate from all its neighbours, is joylessly displayed. Here four girls sit tense over their sewing machines, silent and unsmiling, motionless but for the quick twist and tug of their fingers. There a solitary shirtsleeved man is hunched over his files and calculators, beneath the dazzling light of his naked bulb, dead to all else and perhaps to himself. Along the way eight or nine families seem to be packed into one room, and one sees only flashes of infant limbs, waves of drapery, buckets, black loose hair, bedclothes and grinning mop faces, as though some perpetual and appalling farce is being played inside.

Every room there is ablaze, every room full; and across the gloom one hears radios, clicking machines, shouts and children's screams. In another city all that life over there might be a comfort, a reminder that if you happen to be alone that night, all around you is the warmth of community. In Hong Kong it is different. Nobody in that building seems to take the slightest notice of anyone else – let alone of you as, peering out of the night, your wan Western face gazes aghast across the chasm.

Dead guys

~~

I stood on the edge of Arlington National Cemetery in Washington, DC – Fame's Eternal Camping Ground, as it says on its triumphal arch – and looked across the massed ranks of the departed, like a vast city of slabs. 'Are all these,' said a child beside me, surveying Fame's Eternal Camping Ground herself, 'are all these *dead* guys?' 'Dead,' said I, 'as mutton' – but at that moment her grandmother arrived, and throwing me a distinctly accusatory look, as though I were undermining the loyalty of the young, she gave the child's nose a necessary wipe of the Kleenex and hurried her down the hill to catch the Tour-Mobile.

Duke of London

As it happened the only time I ever saw Winston Churchill was at the very moment of his ultimate triumph – the moment when, on the day of German surrender, he appeared on a balcony in Whitehall to accept the gratitude of London, his battered capital of victory. All around us were grand old monuments of English history, Parliament and Abbey, Nelson on his column up the road, Admiralty and Banqueting Hall and Horse Guards Parade, and it seemed to me then that he was already one of them – so perfectly did his portly smiling presence up there seem to satisfy the setting, the story and the meaning of the day. I always thought he should have been made Duke of London.

Magic in Paris

Wandering into Notre Dame on a Sunday night, I found a choir and orchestra celestially performing Bach's Christmas Oratorio. The cathedral was full, a reverent multitude of young people sitting on the floor if they could not get a seat in the nave, or simply milling about like me. It was magical. All Paris seemed to be there, singing its heart out or half lost in the marvel of it all. When I discovered that the choir and orchestra came from Germany, and realized that half the listeners were as foreign as I was, it only seemed more magical still.

Insufficient compassion

Scary beggars used to infest the centre of Alexandria. I was walking home in Alex one evening when I felt, rather than actually saw, a legless beggar observing my passage from across the street. He was strapped to a low wooden trolley, which he pushed along with his hands, and made an object at once heart rending and frightening to see: but I had no money with me, neither a pound nor a piastre, so I quickened my step self-consciously and hurried down Zaghloul Street towards my hotel.

Behind me I could hear the whirr of his roller-skate wheels as he pursued me through the town – a thump when he eased himself off the pavement, a clanking when he crossed the tramlines, a change of pitch when he left the tarmac for the flagstones. Faster and faster I walked through the evening crowds, but I could never escape those whirring wheels: over the low wall into Zaghloul Square, across the little garden, and I could still hear them skidding down the path, closer than ever behind my back, so that I could hear the poor man's panting breath, too, until at last, breaking into a run, I threw myself into the revolving door of the Cecil.

The wheels came to a sudden stop on the sidewalk outside, and a curse bade me goodnight.

Dignities

In the last years of the Iraqi monarchy the real power behind the throne was the Crown Prince Abdul Illah, a sallow but handsome man. I interviewed him once. He talked fluently and amusingly, and our conversation turned to the pictures on the palace wall, a galaxy of chieftainship. 'What a splendid costume it is,' I said of a portrait of the great Feisal I in Arab dress. 'Do you ever wear it yourself?' 'Sometimes,' said the Crown Prince. 'You would be surprised how comfortable it is.' 'And it does make one look so fearfully dignified,' I said lightly. This was not a success. A chill seemed to settle upon our encounter, and the interview soon ended. The Crown Prince Abdul Illah, it seemed, needed no romantic trappings to give him dignity.

Iddums-diddums

Come with me, and watch a full-blooded beldame selling fish upon the waterfront of San Sebastian. She is flanked by cronies, sitting brawnily on kitchen chairs like a gangster's bodyguard. She herself stands in the middle with a microphone around her neck, wearing a blue anorak, a pink chiffon scarf, white ankle socks and a suggestion of innumerable underclothes. She looks as though no nuance of life has escaped her. Her face is heavy jowled, her wrists are muscular, and she is built like a boxer, but there is a rich urbanity to her voice as she intones the price of sardines. The crowd is altogether at her command. The seamen stumble in with their fish trays like acolytes in an archiepiscopal presence.

The cronies laugh at her every joke. Policemen sheepishly perambulate. Customers never dare to argue. But sometimes that empress of the fish market, pausing to scribble a price upon her pad, notices a baby in somebody's arms, and looks up unexpectedly with the sweetest of grandmotherly smiles, a twiddle of cod-scaled fingers and what I take to be the Basque equivalent of 'Iddums-diddums.'

In the park

I woke early and walked across Chowringi into the green of Calcutta's Maidan, before the sun rose and the heat haze fell like a web upon us. It was lovely then in the park. Rooks cawed, kites hung, sparrows pecked, smiling pi-dogs padded by. Here and there across the grass white figures moved or loitered, and whenever I paused I was sympathetically accosted. 'What you are seeing is the Theatre, built in honour of our great poet Rabindranath Tagore.' 'If I may say so you would be more comfortable where there not so many ants.' Or: 'Wouldn't you like a game of golf? I am teaching golf, you see. Here are my golf clubs.'

Tradition

'Does he, do you think,' tactfully inquired the Bishop of Barrackpore, 'expect a T-I-P?' But no, my guide was not ready for one yet, having high hopes of further services to be performed, so I joined the bishop on his verandah, where during a lull before evensong he was eating peanut butter sandwiches with a kind Anglican lady in blue. He was all an aficionado of the tradition could ask: cassocked, distinguished, fatherly, concerned about that T-I-P. Soon, he told me, he would be retiring. Going home? I wondered, but as the lady replaced the tea cosy with a significant air he answered me in grave italics: 'Staying in India – *for ever.*'

At evensong we sang the hymn that says the Lord's throne shall never like earth's proud empires pass away, and as I left the cathedral a Balliol voice called kindly across the transept – 'I say! Excuse me! You do know where we are, don't you, if you're coming to the children's dance drama in the parish hall?'

Arrival of the tourists

Down in the harbour of Capri I can see the morning vaporetto from the mainland, still hazy about the funnel, and here flooding into the piazza, pouring out of taxis, out of buses, out of horse carriages, out of the steep funicular that runs up from the waterfront – wearing floppy straw hats and rope-soled shoes and pink jeans and multifarious bangles – festooned with cameras, inquiring the price of swimsuits, unfolding maps, touching up their lipsticks beneath the campanile – talking German, English, French and every variety of Italian – young and old, blatant and demure, strait laced and outrageous, earnest and frivolous and thrilled and sick-to-death-of-it-all – here past my cafe table streams the first quota of the morning's tourists.

Teatime in Old Chicago, 1950s

I love to watch the customers at a carriage-trade Chicago restaurant at English Teatime, with Jasmine Tea and Toasted Muffins beside the goldfish pool. Its children behave with almost fictional decorum. Its daughters wear pearls. Its young mums look as though they have come direct from committee meetings of charitable balls. Its husbands look as though they keep fit by riding hunters through parks before breakfast. Its grandmothers, best of all, talk in throaty turtle voices, as though the words are being squeezed out from beneath the carapace and they are heavily loaded with inherited gewgaws, and are inclined to call the waitress 'child', as though expecting pretty curtseys in return. 'Would you care for some more Jasmine Tea, Mrs Windlesham? Do you desire another Toasted English Muffin?' 'Why thank you, child – how pretty you are looking today!' 'Thank *you*, Mrs Windlesham, it's always a pleasure to serve you and the members of your family.'

A separate sphere?

One evening at Akureyri, on the northern coast of Iceland, I heard the sound of solemn singing from a restaurant, and peering through its door I saw that a large party was in peculiar progress. I felt as though I were looking in at some utterly separate sphere of existence. There the Icelanders, men and women, sat in ordered ranks, their arms linked around the long tables, and as they sang what seemed to be some kind of sacramental anthem they swayed heavily from side to side in rhythmic motion. The sight of them gave me a queer sense of secret solidarity. Everybody clearly knew the words of the song, and the whole assembly seemed to be in some sort of arcane collusion. I noticed that if ever I caught an eye, as the celebrants sang and swayed there at the table, after a moment's puzzled focusing it abruptly switched away from me, as if to dismiss an illusion.

'Are they?'

Every evening at the Pera Palace Hotel in Istanbul a string trio plays, attentively listened to by the German package tourists at their communal tables, and gives the place a comfortable, palm-court air. Two elderly gentlemen in Gypsy outfits are on piano and accordion, and they are led by a romantic Gypsy fiddler, adept at waltzes and polkas. I was sitting there one evening when suddenly there burst into the room, driving the trio from its podium and severely disconcerting the hausfraus, a team of ferocious Anatolian folk dancers, accompanied by a young man with a reedy trumpet and an apparently half-crazed drummer. The dancers were fairly crazed themselves. Apparently welded together into a multicoloured phalanx, they shrieked, they roared with laughter, they leapt, they whirled, they waved handkerchiefs – a performance of furious bravura, leaving us all breathless and aghast. They were like so many houris, come to dance over the corpses on a battlefield.

They withdrew as abruptly as they had arrived, and in the stunned hush that ensued I turned to the Americans at the next table. 'My God,' I said, 'I'm glad they're on our side!' But a knowing look crossed the man's face. 'Ah, but *are* they?' he replied.

Tyrant

⌐⌐

A terrifyingly ambitious, inexhaustible girl supervisor works at one of the downtown McDonald's of Manhattan. Over the serving counter one may see the glazed and vacant faces of the cooks, a black man and a couple of Puerto Ricans, who appear to speak no English; in front that small tyrant strides peremptorily up and down, yelling orders, angrily correcting errors and constantly falling back upon an exhortatory slogan of her own: *C'mon, guys, today guys, today* . . . The cooks look back in pained incomprehension.

Divine merriment

⌐⌐

We find ourselves lost on the edge of a deserted traffic junction somewhere east of Kranj, Slovenia. Helplessly we consult our map, hopefully we look for somebody to ask the way, and presently there somehow seem to sidle into our company half a dozen Slovene men and a very talkative Slovene woman. Between us we speak five languages, but we are fluent only in our own, and gradually our discussions descend into farce. It's that way, for sure, no it's the other, they haven't been through Preddvor, no, no of course they haven't, they came the Cerklje way – they should go back the way they came then, they should have gone by Duplice – no, no, no, look here, look at the map – and so, as the map gets

129

more and more crumpled, the arguments louder, the languages ever more incomprehensible, we subside into impotent merriment, shake hands with each other, clap one another on the back and, chuckling still, go our various ways. We ourselves are no wiser about our situation, so we leave the car on the grassy verge and go for a drink instead.

God habitually smiles upon Slovenia, and sometimes he laughs out loud.

Violetta down under

Go to *La Traviata* at Sydney Opera House and, my, what a robust Australian chorus will be attendant upon Violetta in the opening act, their crinolines and Parisian whiskers delightfully failing to disguise physiques born out of Australian surf and sunshine – while even La Traviata herself, as she subsides to the last curtain, may seem to you the victim of some specifically Australian variety of tuberculosis, since she looks as though immediately after the curtain calls she will be off for a vigorous set of tennis with the conductor, or at least a grilled lobster with orange juice and caramel.

The Leading Citizen's lesson

'Have your fun, Jan,' said the Leading Citizen. 'Sure thing, this is a Fun Town, but what we especially do not like is these comparisons with Sodom and such. What people forget is that here in Las Vegas we have a thriving civic-minded community. We have 130 church buildings, Jan, in this city of ours. I think I could safely say that you won't find a more lovely home environment anywhere than some of our high-grade home environments here. What I want you to remember, Jan, is this – the Spanish Trail came this way, right over this very spot, before the game of roulette ever entered the Infant Republic – that's what I always tell people like you, who come inquiring – before the game of roulette ever entered the Infant Republic of the United States!'

The Very Reverend

Almost at once I met the Dean of Wells, actually in the shadow of Penniless Porch. Eton, Oxford and the Welsh Guards, he was not hard to identify. With a splendid concern his voice rang out, as we sat there watching the citizenry pass by. 'Good morning, good morning! Lovely day! What a success yesterday – what *would* we have done without you? Morning, Simon! Morning, Bert! Morning, John! (*John Harvey, you know, our greatest authority on church architecture . . .*)' In his cathedral, I was later disconcerted to learn, they habitually call him 'Father', but I certainly could not complain about his authenticity *qua* Dean.

Our Gracie

On a bus in Capri I chanced to meet, I can't remember how, a man who introduced himself as Boris Alperovici, the third husband of Gracie Fields. She was a famous star of the past, a Dame of the British Empire – 'Our Gracie', formerly a household name in her native England but by then somewhat forgotten. She was living in elderly retirement in her villa on the island. Boris took me along to visit her, and she received me graciously, and told me anecdotes of her theatrical life, and had coffee served to me by her seaside swimming pool. It was just as though the old lady were some great Hollywood actress at the height of her career, and she evidently enjoyed it as much as I did. When I got back to Britain I was surprised to meet other people, too, who had chanced to encounter Signor Alperovici on the Capri bus, but couldn't quite remember how, and had sat drinking coffee at the feet of Our Gracie.

The exchange

Wandering around the purlieus of the High Court in Madras, I took out my tape recorder to remind myself of some of its architectural peculiarities. At once I heard an admonitory clapping of hands, and a policeman with a nightstick beckoned me over.

'What have you got there? What is this machine?'

'It's a tape recorder.'

'What are you doing with it here?'

'I am reminding myself of some architectural peculiarities.'

'How do I know it is not a bomb?'

'You can speak into it yourself.'

'What shall I say?'

'Anything.'

'I cannot think of anything to say.'

'Sing a song then.'

'What kind of a song?'

'A Tamil song.'

'Very well, I will sing you a very old Tamil song, a tragic song' – and half closing his eyes, and assuming an unmistakably tragic expression, there in the sunshine outside the court in a high wavering voice he sang several verses of a very, very old Tamil song. I played it back to him.

'Very well,' he said, 'now you have my voice. What will you give me in return?'

But, bless his heart, I was gone by then.

Temper of the South

The temper of the South is inescapable in Houston. You can sense the swagger of it in the postures of the cattle people come into town for dinner or convention: hulking rich men in Stetsons and silver belt buckles, paunchy with their generations of beer and prime steaks, lacquered observant women in bangles, talking rather too loud as Texans are apt to, the wives greeting each other with dainty particularities (*'Why, hi, Cindy. My you're looking pretty!'*) the husbands with spacious generics ('Well, boy, what's things like in East Texas?')

And you can sense the poignant charm of it in the faded white clapboard houses of the Fifth Ward, stilted above the dust of their unpaved streets. There the black folk still idle away the warm evenings on their splintered porches, as in the old story books; there the vibrant hymns still rise from the pews of the Rose of Sharon Tabernacle Church; there the garbage still blows about the garden lots, and you may still be asked, as I was, if, 'Say, ain't you Miss Mary's daughter from the old store? Bless your heart, I used to be one of Miss Mary's best, *best* customers . . .'

Monty

Late one evening during World War II I was walking up Arlington Street towards Piccadilly when there emerged from the door of the Ritz General Sir Bernard Montgomery (not yet a Marshal or a Lord). A policeman saluted as he scuttled down the hotel steps and into his waiting staff car, but I thought there seemed something almost furtive about his movements. I expect he was really in haste to get back to the War Office, or even into battle, but if he had been another kind of general I would have guessed he was hurrying to an assignation down the road in Soho!

Confrontation

Through the crowd waiting for their luggage at the Toronto airport carousel there staggered ever and again a middle-aged woman in a fur hat and a long coat of faded blue, held together by a leather belt evidently inherited from some earlier ensemble. She was burdened with many packages elaborately stringed, wired and brown-papered, she had a sheaf of travel documents generally in her hands, sometimes between her teeth, and she never stopped moving, talking and gesticulating. If she was not hurling questions at expressionless bystanders in theatrically broken English, she was muttering to herself in unknown tongues, or breaking into sarcastic laughter. Often she dropped things; she got into a terrible mess trying to get a baggage cart out of its stack ('You – must – put – money – in – the – slot.' 'What is slot? How is carriage coming? Slot? What is slot?') and when at last she perceived her travelling accoutrements – awful mounds of canvas and split leather – erupting on to the conveyor, like a tank she forced a passage through the immobile Canadians, toppling them left and right or barging them one into another with virtuoso elbow work.

I lost sight of the lady as she passed through customs (I suspect she was involved in some fracas there, or could not undo the knots on her baggage), but she represented for me the archetypal immigrant, arriving at the emblematic immigrant destination of the late twentieth century, and I watched the confrontation with sympathy for both sides.

The spy's discomfort

Roller skating was then all the rage around the Lake of Geneva. Whole families skated along the promenade. Dogs rode about in rollered baskets and youths whizzed shatteringly here and there, scattering the crowds with blasts of the whistles that were held between their teeth. I lunched with a spy of my acquaintance. What kind of a spy he is, who he spies for, or against, I have never been able to discover, but he has all the hallmarks of espionage about him, divides his time between Switzerland and the East, wears raincoats and speaks Greek. We ate little grilled fish at the water's edge and discussed the state of the city. Uncomfortable, he thought it, and getting worse. Security getting tougher? I conjectured. Banks turning difficult? Opposition hotter? No, no, he said testily, holding his hands over his ears, nothing like that: only those damned roller skaters.

Admiral's walk

Split in Croatia is a naval base, and when I was driving out of town I stopped at the traffic lights near the fleet head-quarters. A very senior naval officer started to cross the road. He was loaded with badges, braid and medal ribbons, but wearing as I was a floppy old hat and a less than spotless blue shirt, just for fun I saluted him. His response was Split all over. First he faltered slightly in his steady tread. Then he brought his hand to the peak of his cap in a guarded and cautious way. And then, as the lights changed, I started forward and he scuttled with rather less than an admiral's dignity to the safety of the opposite pavement, he turned round, all rank and propriety discarded, and shared my childish laughter.

True gents

At Three Rivers, stopping for a hamburger, I found that I had locked my car keys in the boot. Small-town Texas swung instantly to my rescue – well, eased itself slowly off its cafe stools, tipped its Stetsons over its eyes, strolled into the car park and stood meditatively eyeing the problem, saying things like *Huh* or *Kindova problem there.* In easy stages they approached the task, sniffing it, feeling it, and when in the end they got the hang of it, enlarged the right aperture, unscrewed the right screws, and found that the keys were not in the boot at all, since I had left them on the Dairy Queen counter, they seemed not in the least disconcerted. Deftly reassembling the mechanism, tilting their Stetsons back again, they drifted back into the cafe murmuring, 'You bet, lady, any time.'

The Low Riders

In Santa Fe the Spanish culture is relentlessly pressed upon by all the influences and temptations of the American Way. Often in the evenings the cultists called the Low Riders cruise through town. They are the public faces, I suppose, of young Hispanica, and as they drive slowly about the streets in their weirdly low-slung limousines, wearing wide hats and dark glasses, radios booming, unsmiling, proud, *stately* one really might say, who knows what resentments or aspirations of their race they are trying to declare?

The call of conscience

On the Bund in Shanghai one evening a youth with the droopy shadow of a moustache confronted me with a kind of dossier. Would I go through his examination paper for him, and correct his mistakes? But I had been pestered by students all afternoon, and I wanted to go and look at the silks in Department Store No. 10. 'No,' said I. 'I won't.'

At that a theatrical scowl crossed his face, screwing up his eyes and turning down the corners of his mouth. He looked then, with that suggestion of whiskers around his chin, like a Chinese villain in a bad old movie, with a gong to clash him in. I circumvented him nevertheless and, ah yes, I thought, if the Gang of Four were still around, you would have me up against a wall by now, with a placard around my neck and a mob to jeer me, not to consult me about participles.

But my conscience pricked me, and I went back and corrected his damned papers after all.

A lesson

I helped a blind lady over a street crossing near the Gare de Lyon. She looked particularly irritable, cross and demanding, but though born and bred in the 12th arrondissement, turned out to be diffidently gentle. It was a lesson to me not to misjudge the hard-mouthed, sharp-eyed, fast-shoving, middle-aged Parisian housewife. I took the lady first to the post office, then to the pharmacy, and when I left her she said: 'Now I give you back your liberty.'

After a Mexican dinner

Theatrical characters, it seemed to me, filled the main square of Oaxaca when we strolled down there for a drink after dinner: nut-brown women cloaked in red, and dapper old gents with silvery moustaches, and gaggles of students like opera choruses, and small policemen with nightsticks, and rumble-tumble infants everywhere, and a blind guitar player doing the rounds of the coffees shops, guided by his urchin familiar, and a gringo hippie or two, and barefoot families of peasants loaded with shopping bundles and making, I assumed, for the mountains. The faces were mostly dry and burnt. The movements seemed kind of airy, as though tending towards weightlessness. Among the trees some children were blowing up long sausage balloons and letting them off with a squirt of air into the night sky, where they rotated dizzily off into the darkness like so many flying serpents.

Harry's

It was in 1946, when the war in Europe was hardly over and Venice was still under the control of the Allied armies, that I first poked my nose through the doors of Harry's Bar in Venice. I was in my twentieth year, and did not know what to expect. The room was smallish and unexpectedly cosy. At the tables were smoky looking, hooded-eyed, tweedy, sometimes hatted, heavily made-up but rather weatherbeaten persons I took to be members of the Italian aristocracy. Sitting at the bar were three or four officers, the British looking disconcertingly suave to me, the Americans dauntingly experienced. The conversation was low but intense, and everyone looked up as I made my entrance. The officers looked up in a cool, officer-like way, holding their glasses. The patricians looked up patricianly, rather disappointedly, as though they had been hoping for better things. But it was the contact I made with the three pairs of eyes behind the counter that I remember best – the eyes of the boss sitting behind his cash till, the eyes of the two busy barmen in their white jackets. The expression in their gazes seemed to me generic to the place. It was at once interested, faintly amused, speculative and all but collusive. It put me simultaneously at my ease and on my guard, made me feel in some way a member of the establishment, and has kept me going back to Harry's from that day to this.

Only in London

I was sitting over my croissant and the morning paper in a coffee shop in Marylebone High Street when a tall elegant man in late middle age walked stiffly in and ordered a cup of coffee. He wore a long dark coat and a trilby tilted over his brow, and I rather think spectacles were inclined towards the end of his nose. He looked to me as though he had enjoyed perhaps rather too good a dinner the night before, but he emanated an air of unconcerned, if not actually oblivious, composure. I put him down for some mildly eccentric and very likely scholarly earl, of the Irish peerage, perhaps, and thought to myself that only in London could one still see such a genial figure, at once so urbane and so well used, more or less direct from the eighteenth century.

'Know who that was?' said the proprietor, when the man had walked perhaps a little shakily out again. 'That was Peter O'Toole. Remember him in Lawrence of Arabia?'

No thanks

I went to a place on the Rio Grande which was, I was told, a
favourite place for illegal immigrants to cross into the
United States. There were a few houses nearby, grazed about
by goats, guarded by many dogs, but I found it a chill and
spooky spot. It seemed full of secrets, and sure enough one
of the neighbours told me that almost every night of the year
people from the south clandestinely crossed the river there,
and crept damp and dripping through the shrubbery into
Texas. 'You see that forest there,' my neighbour said, pointing
to a confusion of shrubbery beside the water. 'I'll bet you
there's people laying there this very minute, waiting for dark,
bad men some of them, from far, far away.' I peered at the
bushes through my binoculars, hoping to see glints of
weaponry, the smoke of marijuana rising, blackened faces
peering back at me through the leaves. All seemed deserted,
though. 'Want to go over and see? See if there's men there
now?' asked my informant helpfully. 'No, thanks,' I said.

Glaswegians

George Square in Glasgow has a family feel to it. People talk
to each other easily on benches. People share gambles, com-
pare prices, take their shoes off to give their poor feet a rest.
The five-year-old boy riding his motorized buggy around the
benches smiles indiscriminately at us all as he blasts past yet
again, and his father proudly tells us how much he paid for
the machine. Sitting there among those citizens, looking at
the civic statues, cursing the buggy boy, while the big buses

slide around the square and the City Chambers look paternal-istically down at us, I seem to feel a comforting sense of community. Ay, well, responds a freckled woman sitting beside me, that's all very well, but life's not all statues in George Square – and what's a wee bairn doing with a contraption like that anyway, he'll do himself a damage in the end.

Wildlife

~⌒~

While searching unsuccessfully for kangaroos in the bush of Mount Ainslie, a wooded hill rising immediately above Canberra, I felt a sudden need to relieve myself. I was just doing so when I heard a padding and a shoving and a rustling through the bushes. Kangaroos at last? Very nearly. Crashing among the branches, as I was in the very act, a few feet away from me there appeared a very large, very bearded, white-shorted and energetically sweating Australian, doing his daily jog, I suppose, during the luncheon break from his duties as Executive Officer Grade Two in the Department of Inter-Administration. 'Ho, ho, ho,' was all he said, as he bounded distinctly roo-like past.

Two in the morning

~⌒~

At two in the morning I decided that enough was enough, and clambering upstairs I knocked upon the door of M. le Propriétaire's private apartment. It sounded as though they were having a football match inside and, sure enough, when the door opened it was the hotelier's three-year-old son, all flushed and tousled with hilarity, who first poked his nose through the crack. 'A million pardons, madame,' came his father after him. 'How can you forgive us? We were having – how do you say it – a little practice match!'

Two Berlins

'I'm the Boss' was the first T-shirt slogan I saw, on the ample bosom of a housewife dancing a vigorous jig with her decidedly un-henpecked husband. East Berlin was having a public holiday, and at the hotel beside the lake several thousand citizens, great-grandmothers to babes in arms, were enjoying a family feast in the sunshine. How genially they laughed, danced, sang, drank their beer and ate their pickled pork knuckles! With what indefatigable smiles the two bands alternated, one with the old oom-pah-pah, the other exploring the less raucous fringes of rock!

That same evening, al fresco in the Grünewald woods on the other side of Berlin, I observed two middle-aged ladies, mother and daughter, perhaps, sharing delicate jokes over their asparagus, and balancing their purses carefully on the rims of their glasses to stop the chestnut blossoms falling into their wine.

Algérie Française

I stand in the big public forum of Algiers, outside the government buildings, watching the citizenry. The square is packed to suffocation, the crowd spilling away through the pleasant gardens, up and down steps, across neighbouring squares, until it peters away at its fringes into clutches of foot-weary housewives at the tables of deserted cafes. There stand the grim paratroopers, the high priests of mid-century Algiers, dressed in boots and camouflage suits, festooned with tommy guns, grenades and pistols, lounging about in attitudes fearfully tough and jungly, or swapping badinage with the crowd. There are the queer bigwigs of this confused and unhealthy city, hastening up the steps to the Governorate, or briefly appearing upon some flowered balcony: ramrod generals in kepis, greasy double-breasted politicians, wild creatures of the nocturnal right, bearded plotters or fanatic militarists. A sickly cheer greets a token delegation of Muslims: spindly old men with ragged robes and a covey of bewildered white-robed women, with a trilling of high voices and an arabesque of reedy clarinets. Before long that vast crowd, like so many maudlin drunks outside a saloon, is caught up in histrionics, swayed to a man by the querulous, pitiful passions of Algiers – until the whole assembly, with a roll of drums and a sting of hot tears, bursts into the 'Marseillaise', and for a moment all seems clear, all seems honourable.

Allegory in Amsterdam

Standing on a bridge in Amsterdam, I noticed a sleek tourist motor boat, all glass and chrome, gliding down the waterway with a warm hum of diesels. Inside it, snug behind the glass, sat five young Americans in bright open-necked shirts and jeans – servicemen, perhaps, from some air base. They all wore sideburns, and peered through their windows with an air of concentration; and as they passed slowly by, inspecting me, too, as though I were a medieval monument, they emanated a powerful sense of allegory. They were new men in a very old world. Their identity tags flashed at their necks like ritual amulets. They seemed to me like young priests from some distant cloistered seminary, on a mission of dogmatic inquiry.

All American

For me the All American has always been the city bus driver. Since I first saw him clicking that little lever above his change machine, to the tinkle of the nickels and dimes sorting themselves out – since I first heard his timeless response: 'Yeah, lady, get out at City Hall' – since I first plucked up courage to ask him if he could manage change for a ten-dollar bill – ever since I first made his acquaintance he has exemplified for me The American. His slumped shirtsleeved posture over the wheel, the weary reach of his arm towards that change machine, the occasional cursing at a cab driver, the unflustered answering of questions as he drives, his eyes always flicking to the mirror – all are the hallmarks of a man who knows the world for what it is, knows his own city to be its epitome, and has no illusions left. 'So it's a big city? Sure it is. So they're tall buildings? So?'

Dinkum Aussie

In Darwin you may meet the Australian male at his most confident, on the edge of the great Outback. He may be of any age, this dinkum Aussie. He may be a humdrum bank clerk, or a prospector driven wildly in from his shack in the wilderness to squander his money on drink and loose living. Whoever he is, he is magnificent to meet: as free a spirit as you can find in the world today, shackled by no inhibition of class or disadvantage, with little sense of thrift and still less of decorum, no agonizing reserve, no contempt, no meanness. It is as though he has been relieved of the burden of the centuries, strengthened and cleansed by the southern sun, and allowed to begin history all over again.

Suddenly there emerges . . .

Suddenly there emerges from some unexpected alley of Kyoto a vision of the legendary Japan – a geisha in all her plastered glory, moving fast and purposeful towards an assignation. Immensely tall is her mound of hair, jet black and shiny; her face is vivid with white and scarlet, her costume is gorgeous with silks, sashes, the gaudiest of clashing colours and the floridest of patterns; and as she hastens awkwardly down the street, embellished from head to foot with paint and brocade, she seems less like a living woman than some fabulous toy, some last masterpiece by Fabergé, enamelled like a queenly trinket, animated by ultimate refinements of clockwork.

A queen rides by

The people around you seem instinct with an air of happy collusion, as though they all know one another, and are linked in one long line of neighbourly acquaintance from Admiralty Arch to the Palace. The soldiers lining the street look fresh faced and rather touching, the policemen are properly genial, and presently you will see, undulating strangely above the crowd, the head of the Queen of England, in a tricorn hat. You can hardly see her horse for the people, but high above the soldiers and the policemen, as she paces grandly by, you may study her pale face – a sad, antique face, it seems to me at such a moment, young but tired, half commanding, half embarrassed, half person, half idea – a face lined with the blood heritage of Alfred the Great, William the Conqueror, Charlemagne, Roderigo the Cid, Barbarossa and her great-grandmother Victoria, Empress of India.

Saturday lunch in Hong Kong

There seem to be a couple of thousand tables at the restaurant, and at them in uproarious enjoyment sits a vast multitude of Chinese, in families running the gamut from infancy to old age. Nobody is alone. Nobody is silent. The noise is deafening, all that talking and laughter mingling with the clanking of plates, the shouts of waiters from one side of the room to the other, the occasional cries of babies, the sizzling of woks and the Chinese music blaring from hidden loudspeakers. In we go, extremely European, and it is like sitting on the edge of a maelstrom, as we vacantly study the enormous menu (bound in gold and scarlet). But we are offered encouraging nods and incomprehensible explanations from the family at the next table, and we smile ourselves in a baffled and innocuous way across the Chinese mass. In a daze we order, and as by a miracle our food arrives, piping hot and indefinable, and in no time at all we are slurping it happily away, all inhibitions lost, and nodding appreciatively to our neighbours as to the Chinese manner born.

Immigrants

Courtesy of the Department of Immigration, I once stood in the background of an immigration booth at JFK to watch passengers from Europe coming through, and it was revealing to see what emotions passed through their eyes when they noticed me there, looking I suppose like an unusually well-disguised Secret Service agent: suspicion nearly always, ingratiation very often, sometimes a hint of collusion, and occasionally a look I had never encountered before, which I took to be fear. Some of the new arrivals had clearly roistered their way across the Atlantic with champagne and canapés. Others, especially the mothers, the squirmy children, the stout beldames with swollen feet, arrived exhausted at that frenzied airport, into the glaring lights, the unremitting noise and movement of the New World; and as they looked wearily from the immigration officer to me, searching I imagine for some warmth of understanding in our faces, I sometimes thought I detected a flicker of regret in theirs.

The officer treated everyone exactly the same, down to the badinage: 'Oh, please don't look at my picture there, I look terrible.' 'It's like we always say, ma'am, if you look as sick as you do in your passport, you're not fit to travel.'

An ugliness

I was once held up on a seashore track by the unloading of live pigs from the Chinese mainland. This is a familiar ugliness of Hong Kong. The pigs are transported in narrow cylindrical cages of wire or wicker, into which they must be jammed so tightly that they lie there grotesquely squashed and distorted, and frequently in pain. That day they were squealing heart-rendingly as they were bumped in barrows at speed towards their slaughter, and I stood helpless and grieving beside the track. At that moment there came in single file from the opposite direction, on their way home from school, a line of small girls in almost exaggeratedly English uniforms, crested blazers, pleated white skirts, small neat knapsacks their backs. Demurely they filed past, their faces exuding school pride and team spirit: and they took not the slightest notice, as they walked daintily by, of the doomed animals screaming in their torture chambers.

'We'd be famous'

Off the top of a building we fell that day, and sidled across the Hudson River, and in few moments the helicopter stopped, shook itself and gingerly descended a couple of hundred feet. Looking out of my side window I found myself hovering, with a disrespectful clatter, close to the nose of the Statue of Liberty. We hung there for a minute, and the sunshine reflected off the water hung about her head. Then, with a last curtsey, we flew away. 'If we hit her we'd be famous,' I said to the pilot as we darted off. 'What a way to go,' he said. 'I'd be the guy who assaulted the Statue of Liberty, and you'd be instant Shakespeare.' Later I climbed up the statue from the ground, and sympathized with the lady who wrote in the visitors' book that it was 'a nice sight but the stairs weren't that wide'.

Subterraneanism

The station was excavated in the early days of the New York subway system, and suggested to me a particularly cramped and airless cave, or perhaps a sunken submarine. The lady at the booth was elderly and all white, almost albino. Her face was ashen. Her eyes seemed to have no pupils. It was as though she had never in her life emerged into the daylight, but had been born and bred down there. When I asked her how she liked working underground, and whether she did not miss the sun, she was rather affronted. What could I know about it? She had worked in the subway for thirty years, and did not regret a moment of it. She loved the old station, liked to see the trains go by, and had many friends among the passengers; and, sure enough, when a black man walked by he called out unexpectedly to that pallid lady behind her grille: 'Howya doin', ma'am? Keepin' well?' 'I'm fine, Jack, thank you kindly,' she replied. 'Keepin' just fine.'

In Old Vienna

⌒

Watch now – stand back – here come a couple of ministers down the steps from the Council Chamber in the Austrian parliament, portly important men, deep in portly and important matters of state – and swoosh, like a rocket from his office leaps the porter, buttoning his jacket – out of his door, panting a little, urgently smoothing his hair, down the steps two at a go, *bitte, bitte!* – just in time, my goodness only just in time to open the door for Their Excellencies, who acknowledge his grovel only with slight inclinations of their heads, so as not to interrupt the flow of their discourse, as they lumber out beneath the figures of Minerva and her attendant sages to their waiting limousines.

Altercation on the Zephyr

⌒

I had pleasant companions at breakfast on the California Zephyr – a girl from Fresno who had never been on a train before, and two railroad buffs who kept me informed about the state of the track. However, I did have one altercation in the dining car. My ticket, I had been told, entitled me to anything I liked on the menu, but when I asked for cornflakes and scrambled eggs I was told I was entitled to one or the other, but not both. I called for the supervisor to expostulate, but I did not get far. I had got it wrong, the functionary said, not unkindly, and I quote him word for word: 'You're not from this country. You don't understand the lingo.' But the girl from Fresno thought that man had been rather rude, and one of the train buffs offered to share his scrambled eggs with me – only fair, really, because I had already urged upon him some of my Cooper's Oxford Marmalade.

A very Irish lady

A very Irish lady, sitting beside me as the ferry chugged doggedly across Sydney harbour, told me sadly that her car had just been stolen, and deliberately driven over a bluff. Never mind, I said, it was only a thing. Her eyes misted. 'Only a thing! Sure that's the way to look at it. Only a thing! I must look at it that way. God bless you, God bless you for that!' 'God bless you too,' I responded lamely, not knowing, as so often happens in discourse with the Irish, anything better to say.

Liveable city

Following the tourist signs towards the Old Town District and the Chinatown of Portland, Oregon, and expecting the usual harmless flummery of restored gas lamps and dragon gates, I crossed Burnside Street and found myself in a corner of hell. Suddenly all around me were the people of Outer America, flat out on the sidewalk, propped against walls, sitting on steps, some apparently drugged, some evidently about to vomit and nearly all of them, it occurred to me, idly wondering whether it was worth while mugging me as I passed. Portland has repeatedly been voted one of the Most Liveable Cities in the United States, but, thought I, you must choose the right part to live in . . .

A performance in Athens

⤴

On a lovely spring day I climbed the Mouseion hill in Athens, all among the olive trees, to see the celestial view of the Parthenon from its summit. The morning smelt delectably of pines, flowers and dust, and my mind was full of Hellenic glories. Halfway up a Greek sprang from the bushes, opened his mackintosh wide and revealed to me his manly equipment. Well, I supposed, why not? Greek art had been displaying masculine glories for a few thousand years, and for that matter the sentries outside the royal palace, down in the city, were something of a disappointment to one of romantic fancy. Goose-stepping up and down in their full and famous finery, they looked to me less like soldiers of lyrical myth than farm boys in drag – bulging, rather sweaty young men who might easily, in their off hours, mount a performance on the hill of Mouseion.

Positive identification

⤴

I was excited when somebody told me that the bronze statue of Enver Hoxha, the late dictator of Albania, still existed in Tirana, preserved in the Monuments Factory where it had been cast. Not so long before it had been the very centrepiece of the capital, dominating Skanderbeg Square until the rebellious populace toppled it – and him. In a flash I was there, accompanied by a young Albanian engineer of my acquaintance. A watchman directed us to a windowless warehouse, apparently sealed off for ever. 'Enver's in there,' he said.

We circled this gloomy mausoleum until I found a spy-hole between the bricks, and there Enver was, recumbent in the shadows, just his bronze thigh to be glimpsed. It was enough. My engineer positively identified the old monster, and he should know. As a student he had been in the fore-front of the rejoicing crowd when the statue was pulled down in Skanderbeg Square. 'I pissed on it,' he complacent-ly recalled, and you can't get more positive than that.

Last post

Even in the very last days of British Hong Kong one could occasionally see an imperial exhibition of the old kind, bands and sergeant majors shouting, every plume out of its box, judges in wigs and red robes, medals jangling on offi-cers' breasts, swords, white gloves and His Excellency the Governor in full fig. I watched such a parade one Armistice Sunday, from a balcony above Statue Square, and all was as it always was. The commands were barked. The sad old hymns were sung. Trumpets trumpeted. Salutes were salut-ed.

Around the Cenotaph a handful of Europeans, mostly tourists I suspect, stood watching in twos and threes. Just behind them the Sunday multitude of Filipino women was settling down to its weekly jollities, spreading themselves happily on the ground, chattering, laughing, fussing about with paper bags, and beyond them again the life of the great city proceeded altogether oblivious of the few score imperi-alists, with guards and musicians, pursuing their rituals at the war memorial.

Breakfast Cokes

At breakfast in my Lithuanian hotel a long, long table covered with brown velveteen cloth is occupied by twenty young Russian males, while at the end of the dim-lit room there sits alone in silence at her victuals a woman who might be typecast as a lady commissar: severe, spectacled, muscular, her hair in a bun and her skirts long and heavy. A solitary waiter in shirtsleeves serves us – thick black coffee (they're out of milk), fried eggs with peas, black bread and very good cheese. Halfway through the meal we are each given a bottle of Coca-Cola. Most of the men drink theirs there and then, in tandem with the coffee, but I notice that as the lady commissar leaves the room, wiping her mouth carefully with her paper napkin and studiously not looking anyone on the face, she takes hers with her.

Grand cru

Being a crude islander, and an iconoclast at that, I decided to cock a snook. I bought for the first and probably the last time in my life a grand cru Montrachet – Marquis de Laguiche, vintage 1993. I got a kindly waitress in a cafe to uncork it for me, and picked up a hefty ham and cheese baguette to eat with it. 'Kindly direct me', I said to a viniculturist who happened to arrive at that moment in his Range Rover, 'to the exact patch of soil that has produced this bottle of wine.' He raised his eyebrows slightly when he saw its label and the napkin-wrapped sandwich in my hand. It was not much of a day for a picnic, he said, but perhaps the wine would help – and with a wonderfully subtle suggestion of disapproval he pointed me the way to Montrachet. '*Bon appétit*,' he brought himself to say, for your Burgundy wine man is nothing if not gentlemanly.

Through a hole in the wall

I looked through a big hole just hammered in the Berlin Wall, and saw into the patch of no-man's-land beyond. It was littered with rolls of discarded barbed wire, surrounded by ruined buildings and floored with the dismal mixture of sand, gravel and rubble that had resulted from three decades of herbicide – for nothing was allowed to soften the allegory of the Wall. Three East German soldiers were in there, one tilted back on a kitchen chair with his cap over his eyes, the others kicking an old steel helmet around in the dust.

Homesickness

In Moscow I made the acquaintance of Guy Burgess, a renegade British diplomat who had been a Soviet agent for some years but was by then sadly nostalgic for England and his mother. I could not help feeling sorry for him, and we agreed to go together one evening to the Bolshoi. We arranged to meet outside the theatre door, and when I got there I saw him waiting for me on the steps. I waved a greeting as I approached him through the crowd, and he waved a response, but by the time I reached the door he had vanished. I never saw him again.

Grecian collusion

I had taken a room in a private house on the outskirts of Monemvasia, and in the evening I walked a mile or so to a taverna for my supper. It was very full and very lively – local people mostly, with some merry Americans. We drank large amounts of furiously resinated retsina out of metal mugs, and I seldom had a happier evening. In the small hours I staggered up the road again to my lodgings, and my landlady, in a flowered housecoat over her nightdress, pulled back the bars and undid the chains of her front door to let me in. I expected her to be tight lipped and disapproving; instead she greeted me with a sly and knowing smile of collusion, as if she had been enjoyably up to no good herself. I went to bed incoherently whistling, and awoke in the morning fresh as a daisy.

Nothing to say

In the bad times of communism a Polish colleague drove me out to a writers' retreat near Zakopane in the southern mountains, and on the way we were stopped by the police. My friend, a man of great charm and intelligence, did not speak when the policeman tapped on his window. He merely took his driving licence from his inside pocket, tucked a banknote into it and handed it out. The policeman did not speak, either. He had no need to. He just took the note, handed the licence back and walked away. My friend drove on without a word to me. There was nothing to say.

Who cared?

It was midnight, and wartime. Sarajevo, pitted all over with bullet marks, was dark and shuttered, and the airport was closed, but I got a seat on a minibus going down to the coast. There were four other passengers – a Swede, a Finn, a Croat and an Englishman. Behind us a second busload was following us through the night. The snow was deep, every now and then we were stopped at road blocks, sometimes we clattered across a temporary bridge beside a blown-up original. Scattered ruins passed dismally by – house after house gaping in the darkness, with no sign of life but for a single dim light, perhaps, on a ground floor, or a fire burning in a brazier. The awful gorges through the mountains loomed around us, dark and dangerous. At about two in the morning we stopped, and our driver got out and peered rather helplessly into the black emptiness behind him, up the highway banked with snow-drifts. 'What's happening?' said the Englishman in front of me. 'What have we stopped for?' The driver explained that the other bus seemed to be lost: there was no sign of its lights, and he was worried that it might have got into trouble back there. The Englishman stretched, pulled his coat more tightly round his shoulders, and settled down to sleep again. 'Who cares?' he said, but he may have been joking.

Too late

Long ago I came across the ruin of one of the great Anglo-Irish mansions of the old Ascendancy, and paused to imagine all the blithe existence it had once known – hunt balls and elegant dowagers and Etonians larking about with girls in the rose gardens. I remarked to a passing Irishman that it seemed a shame all the festive and colourful life of the house should have come to an end, but he replied, 'Oh, wouldn't you think it was too late for that kind of fandango?' He was right, of course, and years later I came across that ruin again, and found I could no longer hear the hunting horns, or glimpse Lady W's ancestral pearls, still less imagine those young English toffs living it up among the bushes.

City of Art and Culture

So enamoured were the Nazis of Weimar that they erected there one of their most celebrated and characteristic monuments. The site they chose was the lovely hill of Ettersberg, just outside the city, which Goethe had long before made famous – he loved to sit and meditate beneath an oak tree there. On my last day in Weimar I paid a visit to this place, now a popular tourist site well publicized in the town. My taxi driver, a gregarious soul, chatted cheerfully to me all the way. Had I enjoyed my stay in Weimar? Did I visit the Goethehaus? What did I think of the food? Did I know that Weimar was to be the European City of Culture in 1999, at the end of the millennium? Congratulations, I said. Recognition once more for the City of Art and Music. 'Exactly,' replied the taxi driver, and just then we turned off the highway up to Buchenwald.

God bless Swissness!

Halfway through my stay at Weggis I cracked my head open entering the lake for a swim, and had to have it stitched. How glad I was of Swissness then! Calmly and steadily the Herr Doktor worked, assisted by Frau Doktor and by their son the computer specialist, and delicate was his technique, and state-of-the-art his equipment, and whenever I opened my eyes I saw through the spotless windows of his surgery the glistening lake, streaked with leisurely waves and ringed with green hills, like a visual tranquillizer.

Norway, 1950s

Norwegian writers still looked wonderfully writerly then, painters were like painters, middle-aged ladies properly middle aged and cardiganed. I happened in Oslo one night to see some members of a theatre cast assembling for a post-performance supper in a restaurant, and watching their meticulously staged arrivals, their accomplished greetings and their mastery of incidental business was almost as stimulating as seeing the play itself.

Welsh pride

In Argentinian Patagonia, long ago, Welsh people established a colony where they could speak their own language and live in their own way, far from the intrusive English. They called it simply Y Wladfa, The Colony, and a century and a half later, when Welshness was fading there, in a farm on the out-skirts of Trevelin I found a last archetype of its settlers. He was like the smile, as it were, on the face of the Cheshire Cat. Not a soul in his household understood Welsh besides him-self, but they all clustered eagerly around us as we talked – a jolly Argentinian wife, diverse unidentified children and grandchildren, dogs and chickens and a horse tied to the fence; and with his cloth cap tilted on his head, his hands in his pockets, that Welshman of South America touched my heart not with melancholy at all, but with grateful pride to be Welsh myself.

'Ai, ai, ai'

Several times during my stay in Rome I came across a cou-ple of countrymen who seemed, in their quaint fustian clothes and peculiar shoes, to have stepped more or less out of the Middle Ages. They were like substantial fauns, haunt-ing the city out of its remote rural past. These medieval fig-ured seemed to me wonderfully exotic, until late one night I encountered the pair of them anxiously consulting a bus timetable beneath a streetlight in the Corso. Then I realized that in fact they piquantly illustrated the matter-of-factnesss of the city. Nobody took the slightest notice of them, as they huddled there; they looked up and asked me for advice about the best way to get home, but when I told them I was a foreigner, 'Ai, ai, ai,' they said theatrically, like Italians in old movies.

The first of the Morgans

On the land of Mr Harold Childs, a horse breeder of Harolyn Hill in Vermont, is buried the stallion Justin Morgan, the only progenitor of that superb American creature the Morgan horse. Mr Childs kindly allowed me to visit the horse's grave, down the hill below his house, and when I walked back he was waiting for me with a present. It was a short piece of lead piping. 'Now this is true,' he said. 'Just here where we're standing there used to be the stables where Justin Morgan was kept, and when we was digging up there on the hill we found this old lead piping, came straight down the hill here, and a branch of that pipe it came right across the yard here and took the water to the stables. Now that's a fact.

'Now I'm going to give you this bit of that pipe. You can say – and it's true – that Justin Morgan drank from the very water that came through this bit of pipe. You take it away with you, now.' I took it gratefully and I have treasured it ever since. 'I shall mount it on wood,' I said as I started the car to leave, 'and I'll have a card saying "From this pipe drank Justin Morgan, the first of all the Morgan horses".' Mr Childs tipped his hat politely, in the old American way. 'Good idea,' he said.

Hell's traffic

Nobody could be much less Neapolitan than I am, and when at last we reached the hotel, limp with excitement, amusement and exhaustion, and I had paid our driver his exorbitant but entirely justified fare, I told the hotel receptionist that I wanted to go home. 'Don't say that,' he replied. 'Wait till you get up to your room, and everything will seem different.'

So it did. Dusk was falling by then, the harbour was speckled with small fishing boats, and in the distance Vesuvius loomed hazy in the half-light. The docks were full of white cruise liners, and even as I watched one of them slipped away from the quay towards the open sea. For a long time I could see her lights, fainter and fainter to the west – treading her way, I liked to imagine, towards calm realms of order. But it did not make me in the least homesick. The receptionist was right. I rang for a bottle of wine, and we sat there on our balcony in perfect contentment, while hell's traffic snarled convivially below.

Frenchness like a cloak

Nothing had changed in the corner restaurant, the one with the awnings and the menu in the polished brass frame. It remained quintessential France, as we islanders have loved and loathed it for several centuries. Madame remained the epitome of everything false, narrow-minded and unreliable. One waiter seemed, as ever, to be some sort of duke, the other was evidently the village idiot. At the table next to mine sat a prosperous local family out for Sunday dinner, well known to the proprietress and esteemed throughout the community – unsmiling, voluminously napkinned, serious and consistent eaters who sometimes, eyeing me out of the corners of their eyes, exchanged in undertones what were doubtless sly Anglophobics before returning sluggishly to their veal.

I do not doubt the bill was wrong. I am sure Madame disliked me as much as I detested her. The veal was, as a matter of fact, rather stringy. But what a contrary delight it all was! How excellent still the vegetables! How much better the wine in France! How stately that duke! How endearing the idiot! With what real gratitude, evading the final scrutiny of the prefectorial table, and sweetly returning Madame's shifty glittering smile, did I wrap the Frenchness of that cafe around me like a cloak, and return cherished to the autoroute!

They thought not

In Beijing the compound called Zhongnanhai is the very heart of the Chinese communist despotism. Its main entrance is to the south, with two great guardian lions. The Red Flag flies from a mast outside, and within the gate an inner wall is inscribed with the cabbalistic text 'Serve the People'. You cannot see past it, though. Two armed sentries stand there, with two more over their shoulders. They look distinctly unwelcoming, as they stare motionless and expressionless into the street: and sure enough, when I asked them if I could take a stroll inside Zhongnanhai, they seemed to think not.

The Smile Test

The Smile Test is the system I employ to gauge the responsiveness of cities, and it entails smiling relentlessly, if not unnervingly, at everyone I meet walking along a street. I devised it in Vancouver, which remains a good place to test the system. Pay attention now, as we try it out in Robson Street, one of the raciest of the city's downtown boulevards. Many of our subjects disqualify themselves from the start, so obdurately do they decline eye contact. Others are so shaken that they have no time to register a response before we have passed by. A majority look back with a blank but generally amenable expression, as though they would readily return a smile if they could be sure it was required of them, and were quite certain that the smile was for them and not for somebody else. A few can just summon up the nerve to offer a diffident upturn at the corners of the mouth, but if anybody smiles back instantly, instinctively, joyously, you can be sure it is a visiting American, or an immigrant not yet indoctrinated. Whenever I go to Vancouver people ask me how they're doing in the Smile Test. I respond with a nervous smile myself.

Suburban enchantment

In the evening I saw *Die Fledermaus*, staged with a genuine rollicking panache, and so instinct with the magic of the waltz, the whirl of white skirts and the flick of tailcoats, that when I inspected the faces of the women around me, Soviet proletarians every one, I found them glazed with a true suburban enchantment.

GORGE

One person in particular at Iceland, the Sydney skating rink, seemed to me quintessentially Australian. He was about five years old, I suppose, blond, lively, tough and unsmiling. He could not, it seemed, actually skate, but he was adept at running about the rink on his blades, and his one purpose of the morning was to gather up the slush that fell off other people's boots, and throw it at passing skaters. This task he pursued with skilful and unflagging zeal. Hop, hop, he would abruptly appear upon the rink, and, picking a likely target, staggering his way across the ice, inexorably he would hunt that victim down until *slosh!* the missile was dispatched – and hobble, hobble, quick as a flash he was out of the rink again, gathering more slush.

He hardly ever fell over, he seldom missed, and he did everything with a dexterous assiduity. When I asked him his name he spelt out GORGE with his finger on the rail of the rink; when I asked him if he was enjoying himself he just nodded grimly; and in my mind's eye I saw him thirty years from then, exploding into a company meeting perhaps with an irresistible takeover bid, or relentlessly engineering the resignation of a rival undersecretary. I kept my eye firmly on him as I walked out of Iceland, for instinct told me he was assembling slush for me.

Seen from a bus

I sit in a motionless bus near the Sugar Loaf, at Rio de Janeiro, at a place where a small park runs down to the sea. There are military offices nearby, and in constant twos and threes colonels and captains walk by carrying briefcases. My eye is captured, though, by a solitary middle-aged man hanging about at the edge of the park. He bears himself elegantly, slim and erect in a well-cut grey suit, but there is something wrong with him. It seems to be partly physical, partly mental and partly, perhaps, too much coffee. He can never get comfortable. If he sits on a bench, after a moment he gets up again. If he takes a turn around the grass, he abruptly stops. Sometimes he looks up at the hill above, but it seems only to disappoint him, as if he cannot see what he is looking for up there. He inspects the passing officers keenly (was he once a colonel or captain himself?) but he recognizes none. He gazes longingly out to sea, but the sun gets in his eyes. When my bus starts, and we move away from the park, I wave at him through the window, he waves abstractedly back – but not at me, I think, not at me.

Very simple matters

'Certainly,' said the government spokesman, perusing my list of questions. 'By all means, these are very simple matters. We can attend to them for you at once. As I told you, it is our duty! It is what we are paid for! I myself have to attend to an important meeting this afternoon – you will excuse me I hope? – but I will leave all these little matters with our good Mrs Gupta and all will be taken care of. I will telephone with the answers myself without fail – or it not myself, then Mrs Gupta will be sure to telephone you either today or tomorrow morning. Did you sign our register? A duplicate signature here if you would not mind, and the lady at the door will issue you with the requisite application form for a pass – it will make everything easier for you, you see. Have no fear, Mrs Gupta will take care of everything.'

But neither he nor Mrs Gupta ever did ring.

I smell

I drove direct from the horrible purlieus of San Cristóbal, one of the worst of the Lima *barriadas*, to have tea at the Country Club in San Isidro. The odour of the slum went with me, clinging to my clothes and the soles of my shoes like some blasphemous travesty of incense, and as I sat there among the little black dresses and the sticky cakes, the greying distinctions and the foppish playboys, the starched nannies and the exquisite children on the lawn, the chic and the cultivation and the chit-chat of urbanity – as I sat there with the squalor still in my hair I could not help remembering, Pharisaical it seems in retrospect, Dr Johnson's celebrated differentiation, I smell, you stink.

Bastille Day

For hours I had been hanging about the airport at Kharkov, fobbed off by supercilious airline employees through delay after delay in a bitterly cold and comfortless waiting room, until at last the patience of my Soviet passengers expired. They found a boarding ramp, pushed it on to the tarmac, climbed up to the aircraft and, brushing aside the horrified stewardesses, plumped themselves in their seats and called for vodka. I followed in their wake rejoicing, feeling as though we had stormed life's varied Kremlins.

At the trial of Eichmann in Jerusalem

I looked at Adolf Eichmann to see how he was reacting, half expecting to see some flicker of perverse pride crossing his face. But he was sitting well back in his chair, with his hands in his lap, blinking frequently and moving his lips, and he reminded me irresistibly of some elderly pinched housewife in a flowered pinafore, leaning back on her antimacassar and shifting her false teeth as she listened to the railing gossip of a neighbour. It was only towards the end of the morning, several hours, ten thousand words and an eternity of horrors later, that the old lady in the pinny began to sway and fidget a little in her chair, as though she were pining for a nice cup of tea.

Waiting for Churchill

Up on the mountainside, while the press of the world jostle for scoops and angles in the hostelries below, old Sir Winston lies in bed. He lies there in seclusion, the last of the giants, reading his newspapers and confounding his pleurisies while they wait for him to die. Some of my colleagues depict him demanding brandy, puffing cigars, writing his own health bulletins, calling for splendid enormous meals. For myself, when I was up the mountain one evening I thought I heard a sound from the villa, above the sweetness of the birds and the distant sawing of a woodman. It came from an upstairs window and it sounded to me uncommonly like a rich, quixotic, irrepressible, ageless Harrovian chuckle. 'How come you heard that and nobody else? You got influence some place? Hey, garçon, two dries.'

Home thoughts from Barbados

The parishioners who came to the service were nearly all black people, sugar workers and their families from the island estates, but few of them were really strangers to me. Their white muslins and their wide straw hats once graced the English social fabric, and when they sat down expectantly for the sermon the rustle of their petticoats and the crackling of their starch filtered though to me across the pages of many an Edwardian memoir. I knew what hymns they would sing with gusto, for I had heard the same tentative starts and communal diapasons at many a grumbling British army church parade. The verger in his black cassock I had often met before, pointing out the ravages of death-watch beetle in the shires, and when the piano struck up its preliminary chord I knew from her air of proud command which of those old friends would be the one who always comes in half a beat before the beginning of the verse. 'Amen, amen,' murmured the congregation at the end of the sermon, and it was like the clatter of hobnailed boots on the stone-flagged floor of a dairy.

End of a battle

The Israelis had won. Tanks clattered by. Trucks came and went. Soldiers climbed aboard and waved goodbye to each other. It rained, and I prepared to move on too, but just then a rainbow came. 'Look, a rainbow,' I said to a bearded and taciturn sergeant not long from Romania, and added sentimentally: 'Omen of peace!' 'It is not a reasonable analogy to the present situation,' he replied, shifting his Sten gun on his shoulder. 'God showed Noah the rainbow as a promise for no more floods in the future. When He merely wished to show that Noah could now leave the ark, He dispatched a small bird, carrying a piece of tree in its snout.'

Among the treasures

In the vaults of the Central Bank of Persia, before the Iranian Revolution, were kept the priceless and legendary Crown Jewels, in a huge underground strongroom. I was down there one crowded weekday, when it was open to the public, and came across an agreeable case of brooches and little jewelled watches. I stooped to examine them more closely, and as I did so the treasure house suddenly reverberated with the ear-splitting blast of an alarm hooter. Everyone froze. Not a word was spoken. The hooter went on hooting. For a moment nothing else happened, and then a smart young woman in green walked with composure across the room. She avoided the case containing the Gika of Nadir Shah, with its diamond ornaments of bayonets and gun barrels around a monumental emerald. She ignored the sceptre presented to Reza Shah by the people of Azerbaijan, with its gold lions rampant around a jewelled globe. She took no notice of the Sea of Light inherited from the first Mogul Emperor of India. Instead she walked calmly through the room, utterly silent but for the clicking of her heels, directly between the display cases to me. 'May I please ask you,' she said with an amiable smile, 'to remove your elbow from that metal bar around the jewel case?' I moved my arm. The hooter stopped. 'Thank you,' she said, and walked composedly back again.

Affronted

〜

'Those Algerians!' expostulated an elderly politician in Reykjavik, when our conversation turned to politics. He wagged his beard irritably, as elderly Nordic politicians do. 'They're nothing but troublemakers. They were up here, you know, making mischief – Einar Arnarson, I think it was, he put paid to them, he and Jon Olafsson and one or two others' – and suddenly it dawned upon me, as his sharp affronted eyes blazed into mine, that he was talking about the Barbary Pirates.

A lovely dream

〜

The day I arrived in Harar, Ethiopia, I spent a happy hour in the market, sitting beside a courteous silversmith and watching the rural citizenry at its shopping. There was nothing ugly to be seen there, nothing sham, nothing pretentious. It was like watching an assembly of beautiful lithe-limbed animals, so easily did all those people move, so naturally, so discreetly; and as I sat there on my stone seat, the craftsman tinkling away beside me, or engaged in earnest but desultory haggling with half-naked but otherwise impeccable debutantes, I thought how fortunate were those creatures of nature, those children of the thatched hut and the empty places, those sisters of specious innocence. But alas, even there the dream would soon be over.

Fair enough

Would they be casting their votes as Jamaicans, I asked the Kingston Rastafarians, in the forthcoming elections? The idea horrified them. 'Tell your Queen Elizabeth,' they said, 'that the suffering Ethiopians assembled here from the corners of the earth, yea verily from the four corners, it is written, the seventh year of the seventh epoch, yea verily the time has come, Abja! – tell her that we are aliens in this land, and cannot vote in elections imposed upon us by our oppressors. Fair enough?'

Proverb in Formosa

The Vice-President of Nationalist China, in his garden on the island of Formosa, folded his intricate old hands in his lap and projected a Chinese proverb at me. Beneath the trees on the edge of the lawn a stalwart servant waited in attentive silence, and a few soft raindrops were spattering the foliage in a sly, oriental kind of way. 'Among our people we have a saying,' the Vice-President said. '"It is foolish to judge the character of a man by the complexion of his face."' And his pale eyes flickered at me, as an old experienced tiger's eyes might blink in the forests of the night.

Opposite directions

Very early one morning two men met outside my tent on a mountainside in Wales. The younger of the two was a tatterdemalion Welsh shepherd, cloth capped, driving his sheep down to the road with a clatter and scurry, calling to his dog, shouting guttural Welsh encouragements and waving his thick stick like an apparition. The elder, a scholarly looking man in plus fours, was evidently a believer in rhythmic breathing, for as he walked he whistled to himself a monotonous Bach-like melody – two beats to each footstep, round and round, over and over again in an endless classical cadence. The two men passed each other as I gaped at them through my tent flap. The shepherd brandished his stick and grunted casually; the scholar interrupted his fugue to offer a greeting in a reedy academic voice; and so they disappeared into the rain, in opposite directions.

At the theatre

The audience at a Tokyo Kabuki theatre consists mostly of women in kimonos, following the drama with an informed avidity I have seen paralleled only among rugby crowds in South Africa. You sit there wedged between the brocades, baffled by the tortuosities of the plot, swathed in the sickly perfumes of Japan, while high above you in the balcony the narrator declaims his lines majestically from a tasselled lectern. The man beside him plucks dreamily or astringently at his ancient instrument, and on the magnificent stage the queer medieval figures sit and strut and gesticulate with falsetto voices and grand flamboyant costumes. All that is grand, awful or ablaze in the old Japan lives on, twitching and quivering, in the theatre of the Kabuki.

Schooner travel

At Granada the schooner captain kindly signed me on as crew, and to avoid awkward questions stuffed me away in a cubbyhole of his vessel until the heavy footfalls of authority had died away along the quay. When I was released I crept out blinking to find the schooner already scudding gaily out of harbour, and the captain grinning beside the wheel with a tin mug of rum in his hand. African, British, French and Indian ancestors had all contributed to his ship's company, and in the tiny starboard deckhouse, I presently discovered, there resided a seductive mulatto camp follower, immured there silently like a lady about to be sawn in half. We all slept on the open deck, and when the moon came up I heard somebody murmur to this nubile shipmate: 'You got your moonburn lotion, honey?'

The clock and the nougat

'My brother-in-law,' said the woman I had given a lift to, who was dressed funereally and clutched a posy of lilies in a sanctimonious sort of way – 'my brother-in-law has told me that the British are more honest than we Calabrese. Is this so?' I had taken a peculiar dislike to this person, and had noticed that she was eyeing my travelling clock with an interest unmistakably covetous. So when she asked me again, wriggling in her seat in a manner at once obsequious and obscurely arrogant – 'Eh, is it true?' – I answered her harshly. 'Perfectly true,' said I. She was unperturbed. When I dropped her she said nastily, 'Haven't you got some small memento to give me, some small gift or souvenir?' 'Only the memory of our meeting,' said I firmly, shoving the travelling clock out of sight beneath the dashboard – and she shamed me then, by pressing into my hand a large and rather nasty bar of nougat.

The portrait

Brigadier Abdul Karim Kassem has today led a violent coup d'état which has suddenly made him the prime minister of Iraq, and he has invited the gentlemen of the press to meet him at the Ministry of Information. Soldiers stand guard with tommy guns, the Deputy Prime Minister and the Minister of Information (since this morning) are in attendance, and pointedly on the floor of the room is the new leader's camp bed, with a pair of green striped pyjamas folded primly on its pillow. In a corner stands a large, enthusiastic and evidently freshly painted portrait of the brigadier. 'May we ask the Prime Minister', says an American reporter with a courtly air, 'if that is a new portrait of His Excellency, and, if so, who painted it?' The Prime Minister smiles a glittering smile and is silent, so his deputy answers for him. 'Yes, it is a new one. It was painted by the people. It is a present.' 'All the Iraqi people like this government very much,' adds the Prime Minister then. 'Ask the people yourselves. When I go into the street everybody is friendly.' The American clears his throat. The American public would be interested to know, he feels sure, if it is not too personal a question, if any particular one of the Iraqi people painted the portrait, and if so, which? But 'Gentlemen,' intervenes the Minister of Information, 'I think we are all very tired,' so we shake hands with His Excellency and filter through the sentries into the street.

'For heaven's sake'

One Christmas in Vienna I went for a walk in a park before returning to the hotel where my Christmas dinner was roasting. There was hardly a woman in the park. Everywhere the husbands of Vienna, with their children, aimlessly but expectantly loitered, expelled from under the womanly feet of the city while Gretchen and Helga got on with the job. Christmas is a time when old hierarchies are restored. 'For heaven's sake,' I could hear the housewives of all Europe grumbling that day, 'go out and get yourself some fresh air, and take the children with you.'

Wine of the country

The Colonel's family had lived in the same Scottish Lowlands house for several centuries, but as a retired widower he lived unostentatiously, and I was greeted with a homely plate of scones and raspberry jam, and a pot of tea in a blue flowered teapot beneath a bobbled cosy. He ate and drank his ration with enthusiasm, but very soon afterwards fetched a bottle of whisky from the sideboard and poured a couple of glasses – 'Wine of the country – I always say, you should drink the wine of the country.'

He looked like an Irish deerhound, very tall and elongated, his figure only slightly stooped with age, and he was dressed tweedily, with shoes that looked handmade. At first sight he did not appear to be Scottish at all, but after a while, through that expensively anglicized exterior there began to appear something pricklier, more gingery, more ruthless, perhaps, and I realized in fact that I was talking to a man almost aboriginally Scots. His attitudes were mellow. His subjects of conversation ranged from Bonnie Prince Charlie ('All those Stuarts were a rotten lot') to the price of claret ('I used to get it from a man I know in Bordeaux, but now I just go to the supermarket') to snooker on TV ('They're very sporting fellows, extremely sporting'). He alludes now and then to some duke, marquis or other ('by way of being a relative of mine'), but only to tell a comic tale about him, discredit a medieval anecdote or explain the genesis of a portrait. It was raining when I left him, but he came to the bottom of the garden to wave me away, and as I turned the corner of the drive I glanced in the driving mirror to see that old inheritor of blood feud and cattle raid regain the shelter of his door, as though he were escaping a royal posse, in a single mighty stride.

Holy experiences

Consider this family of Irish people, sitting beneath a canopy in the drizzle of a Marian shrine in County Waterford. The image of the Virgin is not very old, but stands strangely half in shadow on a rock wall in a frond-filled grotto, with a stream running below. During the last few months it has repeatedly been seen to move of its own accord, and to be transfigured. Sometimes its face changes into that of Christ, and sometimes it apparently comes to life – early last night, a bright-eyed lady at the gate tells me, she met the Virgin walking silently by the stream. The family sits there, mother, father, adult son and daughter, in a determined common trance, their eyes fixed immovably upon the statue on the rock – willing it to move, praying for a manifestation, clutching rosaries, lips moving sometimes but bodies still as images themselves. They were like addicts at a gaming table. The rain fell all around.

Sacred memories

I went to the 300th-anniversary march of the Prentice Boys in Londonderry (aka Derry), by which the Protestant Orange Order remembers a famous victory over the Catholics, and never did I see such a variety of remarkable faces, pinched, florid, genial or fierce beneath their bowler hats or tam-o'-shanters. Never were pipe-and-drum bands more fervent. Never was I in a crowd so absolutely united in its bigotries. Thirty thousand Orangemen took part in the march, and for five hours an air of perfervid dedication enveloped the city. There were tiny boys of three or four marching with the rest. There were half-crazed bass drummers and clown-like drum majors, juggling their batons, balancing them on the ends of their noses, strutting and ges-

turing like circus performers. There were ranks of stern elderly men, bowler hatted, some carrying swords, all swathed
in the regalia of the Orange Order. Halfway down the procession the hero of the day, a large Presbyterian clergyman,
came swaggering by with a cohort of aides, smiling here and
there and cheered along the way like a dictator moving
among his adoring subjects. Hour after hour the beat of the
drums reverberated, and when I left Derry the Orangemen
were still streaming across the Craigavon Bridge, banners
flying, drummers prancing, strutting infants, determined
old men in medals and bowlers marching in steadfast line
abreast.

Reciprocal ill will

I can see to this day the face of a Benedictine monk I
encountered at the Bavarian monastery of Andechs. In his
late twenties, I would guess, he looked more like an inter-
rogator than a confessor, far more accusatory than forgiving.
Tall, thin, pale, unsmiling, cold eyed, pious as all hell, when I
asked him the way to the monastic cemetery he did not at
first reply at all, but simply turned his cod-like features upon
me with raised eyebrows. When at last he gave me a curt and
loveless answer I hardly had time to thank him (not that I
was planning to be very fulsome about it) before he turned
on his heel with a flounce of his cassock and disappeared
inside the church. I hope he choked on his vespers.

'Oes heddwch?'

Assembled on stage at the National Eisteddfod, the great cultural festival of the Welsh nation, are the Bards of the Druidical Orders, a strange conclave of eminent citizens, doctors and philosophers, writers and politicians, dressed in long hooded robes of white and grey. They are presided over by sages and attended by nymphs in green, by matrons with horns of plenty, by harpists and by trumpeters, and they are there to honour the victor of a poetry competition. The winner's identity is a secret, but he is sitting, we know, somewhere in the audience around us. A hum of excitement and speculation accordingly fills the pavilion. Strange preliminaries occur on the stage: harpists pluck arcane strains, elves dance, a gigantic sword is half drawn from its sheath, then majestically slammed home again. 'Oes heddwch?' cries the Archdruid. 'Is there peace?' 'Heddwch!' thunders back the audience, and the trumpets blow their fanfares, and gathering their robes about them a deputation of Druids gravely leaves the stage to summon the victorious poet to his honours. The organ thunders. A spotlight plays at random over the auditorium. The television cameras are poised in their gantries. The audience strains forward in its seats. Presently the light steadies itself, sweeps deliberately along the seats, and falls at last upon the person of the winner – who, blushing with pride and self-consciousness, and pretending hard to be astonished, allows himself with mock reluctance to be led away by the Druids, up through the huge applauding crowd, up through the reverberating organ music, to the throne that is, for those few moments, the very crucible of Wales. Some years ago I was a member of that Druidical delegation, the man who drew the great sword from its sheath was a famous rugby player and my son Twm was the poet.

Small change

There is a Sydney street group called the Aussie Small Change Brass Band which might well represent the city at ceremonial functions, so alive is it with the authentic Sydney mixture of fun, fizz and chutzpah. Its players are three very small boys in very large hats, with two trumpets, a tuba and extremely powerful amplifiers, and I can tell you they play 'Puttin' on the Ritz' like nobody's business.

Incidental music

I was driving down the Adriatic coast from Istria to Montenegro, and I was playing a recording by Vladimir Ashkenazy of Mozart's 22nd piano concerto. It seemed to me that the vivacious allegro movement of this work absolutely suited the swashbuckling landscape of karst, sea and island through which I was passing, and I drove down the magnificent coast road playing the tape repeatedly, laughing and singing out loud. In the course of the journey I gave a lift to a frail and elderly Montenegrin traveller, wizard-like with stick and black coat, and when towards the end of the journey, Ashkenazy still playing, me still singing, in the delight of my mood I narrowly escaped head-on collision with a convoy of armoured cars, this delightful old worthy seemed to find it just as funny as I did.

The Algerian gardener

⌒

The Algerian gardener at our hotel in the Midi was extremely tall and cadaverous, and his eyes blazed deep in their sockets. His luxuriant sideburns, however, gave him a noble scholarly aspect. He was like a professor in some medieval academy of Islam. As he trundled his barrow about, I used to think, surely he was debating within himself subtle mathematical formulae, or composing Sufi couplets? Once I got up at the break of day, when the place was deserted, and I came across the gardener feeding a black and white cat. He stood very erect above the animal, having placed a grisly dish of offal before it, and I heard him murmuring endearments to the creature. They sounded stately endearments – Koranic, perhaps – and he stood there gauntly as the sun rose behind him, looking down at the cat and murmuring. The cat kept circling around his feet, casting glances at the food, rubbing its head against the man's ankles until it felt it had paid its proper respects. Only then did it fall, with snarls and rendings through its purrs, upon the unlovely victuals.

The matter with me

⌒

'Wazzamatterwidyou?' hissed the angry cab driver, as I stumbled bemused across 45th Street. 'Hey, you in the green hat,' shouts the policeman from his horse, 'can't you see that signal?' 'You must wait for the green,' says the passing lady slowly and sympathetically, assuming I speak only Welsh or Lithuanian, and am new to the mysteries of science. But it takes time to readjust, when you return to Manhattan from idler climes.

To touch the owl

I notice that for mistily religious reasons women in Dijon touch the little figure of an owl in the rue de la Chouette as casually as they might pull on a glove – except that, since it is perched rather high on a wall, small ladies have to jump a bit to reach the bird, and children have to be lifted one after the other, their mothers never interrupting, all the same, the flow of their own conversations.

The friar's warning

At the Capuchin catacombs in Palermo the desiccated corpses of generations of citizens are on display, guarded by friars and climaxed by the body of a child labelled BAMBINA – SLEEPING BEAUTY GIRL. 'Be very careful,' one of the friars said in a flat sort of voice when I left this macabre exhibit – 'watch out for robbers.' I thought there was a queer, occult look in his eye, and hardly had I left the sacred premises than two thugs on a motorbike snatched my bag and left me destitute.

One can always tell

If the hitch-hikers are American I generally stop for them. One can always tell. They try harder for their lifts, holding up well-lettered destination signs and offering ingratiating smiles. They are in the lift-getting business, and they do the job properly. When they are on board they generally work for their keep, too. They tell me all about themselves, they learn all about me, they may give me a brief lecture upon the social customs of my own country, or kindly correct me when I appear to be going the wrong way. They are usually willing to oblige, too. 'Are you going to Scotland?' one young man asked me when I stopped for him just outside London. 'No, I'm going to Wales.' 'OK, make it Wales' – and I drove him all the way to Bala, and left him smoothly chatting up the farmer's wife at a bed-and-breakfast place.

Marvellously goes the elk meat

My favourite place for a Christmas meal is the Operakällaren restaurant in Stockholm. There the restaurant's famous house aquavit is poured most generously by merry waiters of the old school, and everyone soon gives the impression of being acquainted with everyone else. Marvellously goes the elk meat, swiftly pass the herrings, one great salmon succeeds another on the buffet, and very soon I find myself on familiar terms with the Swedes at the next table, complimenting them on their fluent English, admiring little Eva's Christmas frock or little Erik's smart bow tie, exchanging grandmotherly confidences with Mrs Andersson, toasting them one and all with yet more aquavit. Stockholmers are not especially religious people, and I like to think they have been eating those Baltic herrings, downing those fiery liquids, since the days of the pagan kings.

The red tarboosh

Andrew Holden was one of the very last British officials of the Egyptian government, still a highly respected functionary of the Ministry of Finance when Egypt had long recovered its independence. By the time I knew him he was near retirement, but he still went to work each morning by tram, clinging to the outside like any other Cairene if he could not get a seat. The amiable Egyptians, helping him up the step, would make sure he had a place on the rear platform, where he could hang on to the pole, and there I can see him now as the tram swayed and clanked its way into town, so scholarly looking in his spectacles, so slight, so incongruously at ease – and on his head, tilted at a jaunty but not ostentatious angle, the red tarboosh which was the only badge of his commitment.

Dance music

One evening I came across a dance in a Cretan courtyard. The lights were very bright there. The deafeningly amplified music was a quavery sort of oriental theme. A high gate closed the yard, but along the wall of the road above, from windows and shadowy terraces all around, a crowd of villagers watched. Beneath the lights inside, a long circling line of Cretans, men and women, danced a strange dance. I was bewitched. Gracefully, jauntily, thoughtfully, swankily, the dancers tripped their complex steps, and the music blared through the pergola. Round and round they went, to and fro, and sometimes the man at the head of the line, detaching himself momentarily from the rest, threw himself into a spasm, leaping, kicking his feet together, twirling about in an ecstasy of conceit and accomplishment, before the convulsion left him and he subsided into the music's rhythm. When I tore myself away the half-tone music of the loudspeakers tracked me far into the night.

The three days

One of the most demanding of Irish pilgrimages takes the faithful to a grim island in Lough Derg, a remote and dispiriting mountain lake, where they endure a three-day fast, a twenty-four-hour vigil, barefoot peregrinations over stony tracks and the compulsory recitations of 63 Glorias, 124 Creeds, 891 Paternosters and 1,458 Hail Marys. I was once at a wedding at Drogheda, away on the east coast, when I heard a woman ask a worldly young guest with a carnation in his buttonhole and a glass of champagne in his hand where he was going for his holidays that year. I expected Mykonos or Barbados, but no. 'I thought of giving myself', he said, 'the three days at Lough Derg.'

At a Breton window

My small daughter and I looked up from the waterfront of Douarnenez, in Brittany, to see an old woman smiling down at us from an open window. She had a shawl around her shoulders, her face was infinitely wrinkled, and her smile was so kind that it seemed to be reaching us from different times altogether – from before the Fall, perhaps. 'I want that lady,' my small daughter said.

Do I know her?

Now and then I chance to see in real life one of those nameless and numberless actresses of television, encountered in the Underground, perhaps, or browsing at a bookshop. At first I think I really know her. Who could she be? Is she a publisher, or a fellow author? Did we meet on an aircraft, or at a literary festival somewhere? Like one of those nagging fragrances one cannot place, or a tune whose words we can never quite remember, her presence tantalizes and disturbs me. But then with a touch of melancholy I realize that I know her only by proxy, through the medium of the TV screen. Some people in these circumstances introduce themselves anyway, and perhaps one should: I sometimes notice that if I chance to catch the woman's eye she will give me one of those closed-lip actress's smiles, turned up a little too resolutely at the corners of the mouth, as if she is dying to be recognized.

Salon life

A Jewish acquaintance of mine in Delhi, being a passionate horsewoman, established a sort of lien upon the social loyalties of a whole covey of equestrian maharajas, polo players to a man but as fascinated by the personality of their hostess as they were by her love of horses. They became a kind of salon.

They used to sit in her drawing room, itself a strange and wonderful melange of cultures, or sprawl on the lawn with long cool drinks, hanging upon her every word: dark mustachioed military figures, handsome but rather running to plump, and in their midst that small vivacious woman bestowing a chaff here, a compliment there, like a Jewish maharani herself.

Days of liberty!

I chanced to arrive in Paris when a student rebellion was reaching its climax, and was astonished to find the students surging to and fro between their makeshift barricades, handkerchiefs over their mouths, throwing things now and then and shouting slogans. They were all that old people dreamed themselves to have been when they looked back to their days of liberty, the days when they had causes to throw bricks for, when to be alive was grand enough, but heaven itself was to be young, radical, brandishing a stick and shouting a slogan in Paris!

Harry's Challenge

I had a pre-Christmas luncheon at Harry Ramsden's Fish and Chip Shop at Guiseley, where the menu was dominated by Harry's Challenge, a fish-and-chip dish so gigantic that if you got through it you were given a free pudding and a signed certificate. All the customers were the real thing – not another outsider among them, only celebratory office parties hilarious over Harry's Challenge, and amiably extended families with grandmothers in hats, and burbling children with hand-held video games, and not a few stout parties who would have done better to cut down on the steamed ginger pudding. At one o'clock precisely there arrived outside the front door the Scissett Youth Band of Huddersfield, to serenade us lustily with all the old carols – none of your fancy ecumenicals – setting many a sensibly shod foot tapping to their rhythms and inciting me, as an inveterate whistler, to join in messily over my mushy peas.

In other circumstances

Trams are essential to the character of Vienna, but there are some places where they run against the flow of the traffic, and are likely to murder you. When I nearly lost my own life to one of them – *'Quick! Comes the tram the other way!'* – sympathetic onlookers were quick to reassure me that Dr Kurt Waldheim himself had almost died a similar death (although that was of course, they respectfully added, before he became president of our republic . . .)

Below the ships

The longest escalator in Europe plunges beneath the Kiel Canal to take pedestrians to the other side. I stood there one morning looking down this dreadful shaft, which was all empty, dark and rumbling, wondering if anybody ever used it, when a cheerful girl rode up behind me on a bicycle.

Without a pause she tucked the bike under her arm, so to speak, and launched herself upon the moving staircase. I stood there watching her go. Down and down into the dark she went, all alone, smaller and smaller, clutching her bicycle, until she disappeared into the hole beneath the Kiel Canal. Above her the ships sailed on.

Colombian coffee

I once sat for half an hour over a coffee at a pavement cafe in Buenaventura, Colombia, and never did I see a more piteous and dispiriting citizenry pass by, in the sticky blaze of that tropical afternoon. A mutilated beggar crawled about my feet, silently holding out his hand. A shoeshine boy with a withered arm sat listless at the pavement's edge. A few tattered black men slouched about the surrounding tables. Two small boys played football with an old tin in the street. Sometimes a grey figure in white ducks shambled into the cafe, reaching into his money belt for the price of a brandy, sometimes the beggar scuttled off like a huge black crab towards some new arrival, and sometimes the waitress, with a clang of her bangles, screamed some raucous incantation into the kitchen. All around was filth, heat and degradation, malformation and truncation, stumps of arms and crooked arms and scabbed dry lips.

Through a glass darkly

The Yamut Turkoman tribes are the most daunting of the Iranian peoples. On Thursday mornings they hold a horse fair at the village of Pahlevi Dej, and there I went to see them. They converged upon the village in ones and twos, bolt upright on their horses, top heavy in their black fleece hats, in stately lolloping motion across their splendid landscape. Some brought their wives with them, demurely riding pillion and wearing purple or scarlet skirts with brightly flowered shawls. I saluted one formidable tribesman as he rode by; not for a moment did his pace flag, inexorably he continued his progress, kicking up little clouds of dust with each step, and looking distantly down at me from the saddle as through a thick glass plate.

Joking on the coastal route

Once on the *Hurtigruten*, the Norwegian coastal shipping service, an entire brass band boarded our vessel, with musicians of all ages down to small boys and girls. They were going to the next port up the coast and earned their passage by playing sombre but rousing marches in the forward lounge. The faces of the instrumentalists were quintessentially Norwegian: pale, long, incurious, handsome faces. One boy asked me where I was from, and when I told him he said, 'I have a grandmother in Wales.' 'You don't mean it!' I exclaimed in delighted surprise. 'No,' he said, 'I was only joking.'

Pan's blood

Delight is still the occupation of Corfu, and sweet airs of comfort abound. The peasants of old may have deserted their olives for occupations of easier profit, but the olive trees are still there, and the stony earth beneath them, and the scents of herbs in the evening. On our way back from Kavos we saw, in one of the wayside villages, a pick-up truck run over a cat. In a trice the corpse of the poor animal was removed for burial, and I was struck by the air of true sadness that fell upon the village bystanders. It was the sweet silent sadness, I thought, of the ages. When we drove away the little pool of cat's blood left in the street behind us suggested to me the blood of Adonis, or perhaps of Pan himself.

Canadian arrivals

Very early one morning I went down to Union Station to watch the transcontinental train passengers arrive out of the darkness from Vancouver. I knew exactly what to expect from this experience, but still it stirred me: the hiss and rumble of it, the engineers princely in their high cab, the grey faces peering out of sleeper windows, the proud exhaustion of it all – and then the thick tumble of the disembarking passengers, a blur of boots and lumber jackets and hoods and frosty breaths and bags and bundled children, clattering down the steps to breakfast, Grandma and Toronto.

Destiny in Missouri

'Mr Truman? Certainly, he's expecting you,' said the pleasant secretary in Independence, Missouri, and in a moment there was his familiar figure, sitting at a big polished desk. Beside him there stood a large and splendid globe, in a frame stand, and from time to time during our conversation Harry Truman would reflectively spin it or point to parts of it in a manner that I can only describe as proprietorial. He was, as he reminded me, the president who, in the years after World War II, had decreed an interventionist foreign policy for the United States of America – the Truman Doctrine. When he twirled that globe he was retrospectively reshaping my world, abolishing my empire, and affecting the way I would live for the rest of my life.

A cabman's wink

I was wandering the streets of Alexandria's Arab Quarter – 'The best way to see it', E. M. Forster said, 'is to wander aimlessly about' – when I happened to catch the eye of a wrinkled cabby with a towel wrapped round his head, high behind his poor Rosinante on the seat of his gharry. On the impulse of the moment I winked: and instantly there crossed his face an expression of indescribable knowingness and complicity, half comic, half conspiratorial – as though between us, he, the city and I, we had plumbed the depths of human and historical experience, and were still coming up for more.

The touch of a hand at home

The baby, we knew, was very near death.
We lay sleepless in our room overlooking the garden,
and a great moon shone.
Towards midnight a nightingale began to sing.
All night long it trilled and soared in the moonlight,
infinitely sad, infinitely beautiful.
We lay there through it all,
each knowing what the other was thinking,
and the bird sang on, part elegy, part comfort, part
farewell, until the moon failed
and we fell hand in hand into sleep.
In the morning the child had gone.

Index

⌐